AIRMONT SHAKESPEARE

The Tragedy of OTHELLO The Moor of Venice

By

William Shakespeare

General Introduction by Dr. David G. Pitt

AIRMONT PUBLISHING COMPANY, INC.
22 EAST 60TH STREET • NEW YORK 10022

An Airmont Classic
specially selected for the Airmont Library
from the immortal literature of the world

PUBLISHED SIMULTANEOUSLY IN THE DOMINION OF CANADA
BY THE RYERSON PRESS, TORONTO

PRINTED IN THE UNITED STATES OF AMERICA
BY THE COLONIAL PRESS INC., CLINTON, MASSACHUSETTS

GENERAL INTRODUCTION

William Shakespeare: His Life, Times, and Theatre

HIS LIFE

The world's greatest poet and playwright, often called the greatest Englishman, was born in Stratford-on-Avon, Warwickshire, in the year 1564. The exact date of his birth is uncertain, but an entry in the *Stratford Parish Register* gives his baptismal date as April 26, and it is reasonable to assume that he was born on or about April 23—an appropriate day, being the feast of St. George, the patron saint of England.

His father, John Shakespeare, was a glover and dealer in wool and farm products, who had moved to Stratford from Snitterfield, four miles distant, some time before 1552. During his early years in Stratford his business prospered, enabling him to acquire substantial property, including several houses, and to take his place among the more considerable citizens of the town. In 1557 he married Mary, daughter of Robert Arden, a wealthy landowner of Wilmcote, not far from Stratford. Two daughters were born to them before William's birth—Joan, baptized in 1558, and Margaret, baptized in 1562—but both died in infancy. William was thus their third child, though the eldest of those who survived infancy. After him were born Gilbert (1566), another Joan (1569), Anne (1571), Richard (1574), and Edmund (1580).

Very little is positively known about Shakespeare's boyhood and education. We know that for some years after William's birth his father's rise in Stratford society and municipal affairs continued. Many local offices came to him in rapid succession: ale-taster, burgess (a kind of constable), assessor of fines, chamberlain (town treasurer), high bailiff (a kind of magistrate), alderman (town councilor), and chief alderman in 1571. As the son of a man of such eminence, Shakespeare undoubtedly attended the local Grammar School. This he was entitled to do free of charge, his father being a town councilor. We do not know how good a pupil he was nor what subjects he studied. It is probable that he covered the usual Elizabethan curriculum: an "A B C book," the catechism in Latin and English, Latin grammar, the translation of Latin authors, and perhaps some Greek grammar and translation as well. But family circumstances appear to have curtailed his formal education, for shortly before William reached his fourteenth birthday his father's rising fortunes abruptly passed their zenith. About the year 1578, having gone heavily into debt, John Shakespeare lost two large farms inherited by his wife from her father. Thereafter, he was involved in a series of lawsuits, and lost his post on the Stratford town council. Finally, in 1586, he was declared a bankrupt.

In 1582, Shakespeare married Anne, daughter of Richard Hathaway (recently deceased) of the village of Shottery near Stratford. The *Episcopal Register* for the Diocese of Worcester contains their marriage record, dated November 28, 1582; he was then in his eighteenth year and his wife in her twenty-sixth. On May 26 of the following year the *Stratford Parish Register* recorded the baptism of their first child, Susanna; and on February 2, 1585, the baptism of a twin son and daughter named Hamnet and Judith.

How Shakespeare supported his family, how long he continued to live in Stratford, we do not know for certain. Tradition and conjecture have bestowed on him many interim occupations between his marriage and his appearance in London in the early fifteen-nineties: printer, dyer, traveling-player, butcher, soldier, apothecary, thief. Perhaps only the last-named "pursuit" requires some explanation. According to several accounts, Shakespeare fell into bad company some time after his marriage, and on several occasions stole deer from the park of Sir Thomas Lucy, a substantial gentleman of Charlecote, near Stratford.

However he may have occupied himself in the interim, we know that by 1592 Shakespeare was already a budding actor and playwright in London. In that year Robert Greene in his autobiographical pamphlet *A Groatsworth of Wit*, referring to the young actors and menders of old plays who were, it seemed to him, gaining undeserved glory from the labours of their betters (both by acting their plays and by rewriting them), wrote as follows:

> Yes trust them not: for there is an upstart Crow, beautified with our feathers, that with his Tygers heart, wrapt in a Players hyde, supposes he is as well able to bombast out blanke verse as the best of you: and being an absolute *Johannes factotum*, is in his owne conceit the onely Shakescene in a countrey.

"Shakescene" is clearly Shakespeare. The phrase "upstart Crow" probably refers to his country origins and his lack of university education. "Beautified with our feathers" probably means that he uses the older playwrights' words for his own aggrandisement either in plays in which he acts or in those he writes himself. "Tygers heart wrapt in a Players hyde" is a parody of a line in III *Henry VI*, one of the earliest plays ascribed to Shakespeare. And the Latin phrase *Johannes factotum*, meaning Jack-of-all-trades, suggests that he was at this time engaged in all sorts of theatrical jobs: actor, poet, playwright, and perhaps manager as well.

Greene died shortly after making this scurrilous attack on the young upstart from Stratford, and so escaped the resentment of those he had insulted. But Henry Chettle, who had prepared Greene's manuscript for the printer, in his *Kind-Harts Dreame* (1592), apologized to Shakespeare for his share in the offence:

> I am as sory as if the originall fault had beene my fault, because my selfe have seene his demeanor no lesse civill, than he excelent in the qualitie he professes: Besides, divers of worship have reported his uprightness of dealing, which argues honesty, and his facetious grace in writing, that approoves his Art.

Thus, because of an attack upon him by an irascible dying man, we learn that Shakespeare at this time was held in high regard by "divers of worship," that is, by many of high birth, as an upright, honest young man of pleasant manners and manifest skill as actor, poet, and playwright.

Although Shakespeare by 1593 had written, or written parts of, some five or six plays (I, II, and III *Henry VI, Richard III, The Comedy of Errors,* and perhaps *Titus Andronicus*), it was as a non-dramatic poet that he first appeared in print. *Venus and Adonis* and *The Rape of Lucrece,* long narrative poems, both bearing Shakespeare's name, were published in 1593 and 1594 respectively. But thereafter for the next twenty years he wrote almost nothing but drama. In his early period, 1591 to 1596, in addition to the plays named above, he wrote *Love's Labour's Lost, The Taming of the Shrew, Two Gentlemen of Verona, Romeo and Juliet, A Midsummer Night's Dream, Richard II,* and *King John.* Then followed his great middle period, 1596 to 1600, during which he wrote both comedies and history-plays: *The Merchant of Venice,* I and II *Henry IV, The Merry Wives of Windsor, Much Ado about Nothing, Henry V, Julius Caesar, As You Like It,* and *Twelfth Night.* The period of his great tragedies and the so-called "dark comedies" followed (1600-1608): *Hamlet, Troilus and Cressida, All's Well that Ends Well, Measure for Measure, Othello, King Lear, Macbeth, Antony and Cleopatra, Timon of Athens,* and *Coriolanus.* The last phase of his career as dramatist, 1608 to 1613, sometimes called "the period of the romances," produced *Pericles, Prince of Tyre, Cymbeline, The Winter's Tale, The Tempest,* parts of *Henry VIII,* and perhaps parts of *The Two Noble Kinsmen.* Long before his death in 1616 his name held such magic for the public that merely to print it on the title page of any play assured its popular acclaim. The "upstart Crow" had come a long way since 1592.

He had come a long way, too, from the economic straits that may well have driven him to London many years before. We know, for example, from the records of tax assessments that by 1596 Shakespeare was already fairly well-to-do. This is further borne out by his purchasing in the following year a substantial house known as New Place and an acre of land in Stratford for £60, a sizable sum in those days. In 1602 he made a further purchase of 107 acres at Stratford for £320, and a cottage and more land behind his estate at New Place. But his life during this time was not quite unclouded. His only son, Hamnet, died in 1596 at the age of eleven years, his father in 1601, and his mother in 1608. More happily he saw, in 1607, the marriage of his daughter Susanna to Dr. John Hall, an eminent physician of Stratford, and, in the following year, the baptism of his granddaughter, Elizabeth Hall.

Shakespeare's retirement to Stratford appears to have been gradual, but by 1613 he seems to have settled there, though he still went up to London occasionally. Of the last months of his life we know little. We do know that in February, 1616, his second daughter, Judith, married Thomas Quiney. We know that on March 25 Shakespeare revised and signed his will, among other bequests leaving to his wife his "second best bed with the furniture." A month later he was dead, dying on his fifty-second birthday, April 23, 1616. He was buried in the chancel of Holy Trinity Church, Stratford, on April 26.

HIS TIMES

Shakespeare lived during the English Renaissance, that age of transition that links the Mediaeval and the Modern world. Inheriting the rich traditions of the Middle Ages in art, learning, religion, and politics, rediscovering the great legacies of classical culture, the men of the Renaissance went on to new and magnificent achievements in every phase of human endeavor. No other period in history saw such varied and prolific development and expansion. And the reign of Elizabeth I (1558-1603), Shakespeare's age, was the High Renaissance in England.

The universe grew in immensity as men gradually abandoned the old Ptolemaic view of a finite, earth-centered universe, accepting the enormous intellectual challenge of the illimitable cosmos of Copernicus' theory and Galileo's telescope. The earth enlarged, too, as more of its surface was discovered and charted by explorers following the lead of Columbus, Cabot, Magellan, and Vespucci. England itself expanded as explorers and colonizers, such as Frobisher, Davis, Gilbert, Raleigh, Grenville, Drake, and others, carried the English flag into many distant lands and seas; as English trade and commerce expanded with the opening of new markets and new sources of supply; as English sea power grew to protect the trading routes and fend off rivals, particularly Spain, the defeat of whose Invincible Armada in 1588 greatly advanced English national pride at home, and power and prestige abroad.

The world of ideas changed and expanded, too. The rediscovery and reinterpretation of the classics gave a new direction and impetus to secular education. During the Middle Ages theology had dominated education, but now the language, literature, and philosophy of the ancient world, the practical arts of grammar, logic, and rhetoric, and training in morals, manners, and gymnastics assumed the major roles in both school and university—in other words, an education that fitted one for life in the world here and now replaced one that looked rather to the life hereafter.

The Mediaeval view of man was generally not an exalted one. It saw him as more or less depraved, fallen from Grace as a result of Adam's sin; and the things of this world, which was also "fallen," as of little value in terms of his salvation. Natural life was thought of mainly as a preparation for man's entry into Eternity. But Renaissance thought soon began to rehabilitate man, nature, and the things of this life. Without denying man's need for Grace and the value of the means of salvation provided by the Church, men came gradually to accept the idea that there were "goods," values, "innocent delights" to be had in the world here and now, and that God had given them for man to enjoy. Man himself was seen no longer as wholly vile and depraved, incapable even of desiring goodness, but rather as Shakespeare saw him in *Hamlet:*

> What a piece of work is man! how noble in reason! how infinite in faculty! in form and moving how express and admirable! in action how like an angel! in apprehension how like a god! the beauty of the world! the paragon of animals!

And this is the conception of man that permeates Elizabethan thought and literature. It does not mean that man is incorruptible, immune to moral weakness and folly. Shakespeare has his villains, cowards, and fools. But Nature framed him for greatness, endowed him with vast capacities for knowledge, achievement, and delight, and with aspirations that may take him to the stars. "O brave new world, That has such people in 't!"

HIS THEATRE

There were many theatres, or playhouses, in Shakespeare's London. The first was built in 1576 by James Burbage and was called the *Theatre*. It was built like an arena, with a movable platform at one end, and had no seats in the pit, but had benches in the galleries that surrounded it. It was built of wood, and cost about £200. Other famous playhouses of Shakespeare's time included the Curtain, the Bull, the Rose, the Swan, the Fortune, and, most famous of them all, the Globe. It was built in 1599 by the sons of James Burbage, and it was here that most of Shakespeare's plays were performed.

As its name suggests, the Globe was a circular structure (the second Globe, built in 1614 after the first burned down, was octagonal), and was open to the sky, somewhat like a modern football or baseball stadium, though much smaller. It had three tiers of galleries surrounding the central "yard" or pit, and a narrow roof over the top gallery. But must interesting from our viewpoint was the stage—or rather *stages*—which was very different from that of most modern theatres.

The main stage, or *apron* as it was called, jutted well out into the pit, and did not extend all the way across from side to side. There was an area on either side for patrons to sit or stand in, so that actors performing on the apron could be viewed from three sides instead of one. In addition, there was an inner stage, a narrow rectangular recess let into the wall behind the main stage. When not in use it could be closed by a curtain drawn across in front; when open it could be used for interior scenes, arbor scenes, tomb and anteroom scenes and the like. On either side of this inner stage were doors through which the main stage was entered. Besides the inner and outer stages, there were no fewer than four other areas where the action of the play, or parts of it, might be performed. Immediately above the inner stage, and corresponding to it in size and shape, was another room with its front exposed. This was used for upstairs scenes, or for storage when not otherwise in use. In front of this was a narrow railed gallery, which could be used for balcony scenes, or those requiring the walls of a castle or the ramparts of a fortress. On either side of it and on the same level was a window-stage, so-called because it consisted of a small balcony enclosed by windows that opened on hinges. This permitted actors to speak from the open windows to others on the main stage below. In all, it was a very versatile multiple stage and gave the dramatist and producer much more freedom in staging than most modern theatres afford.

The dramatist's words and the imagination of the audience supplied the lack of scenery. No special lighting effects were possible since plays were performed in the daylight that streamed in through the unroofed top of the three-tiered enclosure that was the playhouse. Usually a few standard stage props were on hand: trestles and boards to form a table, benches and chairs, flagons, an altar, artificial trees, weapons, a man's severed head, and a few other items. Costumes were usually elaborate, though no attempt was made to reproduce the dress of the time and place portrayed in the play.

But we need have no doubts about the audience's response. They came, they saw, and the dramatist conquered, for they kept coming back for more and more. And despite the opposition that the theatre encountered from Puritans and others, who thought it the instrument of Satan, the theatre in Shakespeare's time flourished as one of the supreme glories of a glorious age.

—DAVID G. PITT
Memorial University of Newfoundland

INTRODUCTION TO *Othello*

THE TEXT

There exist two early editions of *Othello*. One dates from 1622 in the form of a quarto, that is, with the play published by itself; the other early location of *Othello* is in its proper place among Shakespeare's tragedies in the collected edition of his dramatic works, in the First Folio of 1623. Both are good texts without much visible corruption or error, but neither text brings us very close to the time of its composition and first performance; the earliest record of a performance is from November of 1604. Such a date agrees with what the drama itself would indicate, for this was a time when Shakespeare was preoccupied with the possibilities of the tragic form. At the turn of the century, he had experimented with a type of play that is often labeled a "dark" comedy; without the happy resolution that these plays achieve in the nick of time, it is not a far cry to the darkness of *Hamlet*. With *Othello* there is nothing in the least comic, and the tragedy itself produces one of the most unrelievedly painful effects even when considered alongside the later great tragedies. It is as if Shakespeare intended to examine the limits of tragedy in one particular line of development, as if he wished to demonstrate what the fullest concentration of tragic anguish would reveal, to give us the distilled and most direct force of the form.

Shakespeare's source material in this case gives us the basic facts, but these are more a point of departure for his play than its real origins. From a collection of lurid tales by a sixteenth-century Italian, Giraldi Cinthio, Shakespeare took the account of an unnamed Moor who was married to a virtuous Venetian lady and led astray by a jealous ensign. This officer yearned for Disdemona but, afraid of his chances because of a handsome captain, decided to get the captain removed. The plot he worked is much the same as in the play, except that he has a child steal the handkerchief for him. The actual murder has a grotesque ingenuity to it: the two, the Moor and ensign, beat Disdemona to death with a sand-filled stocking and then pull down the ceiling timbers to hide their guilt. Then it will seem that the Moor's wife was killed by the roof falling in on her. But crime does not pay, though in Cinthio's telling, a good number of added twists and forced confessions and vendettas postpone the day of reckoning. Clearly, the stories are the same but it is scarcely necessary to emphasize the complete separation of the two in any significant sense.

It is true that Shakespeare's source does help create the atmosphere dominant in the play. This is the constant presence of darkness, a darkness that permeates the actions, the characters, the setting, and the meaning of all these in the play. On the most obvious level it is from Cinthio that Shakespeare gets the fact of his hero's darkness. Othello is a Moor, an African who has crossed the Mediterranean, to confront the Elizabethan audience with two things at the same time: the exotic and the paradoxical. To the Elizabethan spectator the figure of Othello was an entirely strange one, and Desdemona is in a sense their (and indeed our) representative in her wonder at her husband's adventures; the less appealing side of this strangeness creates her bewilderment at a man easily given to passionate extremes. Othello's darkness meant mystery to the Elizabethan; it also meant the unknown, the suppressed, the unreasoned. The paradox that this dark, exotic figure raises is also in a way due to Cinthio. Cinthio's story of Venetian crime and its slow, vivid punishment met a receptive audience; this was what the Elizabethans expected of Italy, a strangeness and a menace. Against an Italian background the Elizabethan theatre provided so sensationally and luridly, Othello's honor and trust, and the betraying of these by Iago, emerge as distinctly as possible. Both of these, the African hero and the Italian traitor, are the basic facts of the story of the play. What dramatic elements these facts are made into is the next necessary question; out of these elements are evolved the relationships of character and event, out of them issue the final dramatic consequences, the "tragic" effect of the play. These must be considered, while keeping in mind the ultimate dramatic and even theatrical function and value (and limitation) constant in all of them.

THE DRAMATIC ELEMENTS

The various incidents through which the story progresses and unfolds itself marshal themselves surprisingly neatly, if *Othello* is placed in its proper context of Elizabethan or Shakespearian theatre. In place of the more usual far reaches of time and place (*Antony and Cleopatra* or *King Lear* are perhaps the most extreme illustrations of this tendency), there is an almost classical precision of structure and chain of event. A prologue of one act lays down the necessary conditions: Othello's reputation and value to the Venetian state, his sudden and very recent marriage, and the enmities he is exposed to, some of which he can discount (Brabantio loses his case) but some of which he is not even aware. Iago, Desdemona, and Othello, along with the more subordinate Cassio and Roderigo, are laid down to the audience in clear outline. The remaining four acts are the play; they form one indivisible unit, sharply localized on an island, distinctly marked out in the hours necessary for the action to evolve. There is thus a prologue and the carrying out of its premises to a logical end.

The drama of *Othello* can also be considered classical (to use this much abused term as roughly equivalent to what a critic such as Aristotle would have expected in a play) in the emphasis it allows to plot—and to what sort of plot it, in fact, allows. This emphasis is perhaps best gauged after the play is finished and one thinks back to try to discover what emerges as uppermost, both in the final effect the play leaves and, more abstractly, what has led to this impression. Here the impress is of the events, even more than of the characters who act out or suffer the succession of these events. This seems categorical and is perhaps too baldly put to be convincing; the act and its doer can be only abstractly separated, this for the sake of clearer understanding through analysis. And yet consider the relative difficulties involved in either case if such an analytic division is performed. The characters of Othello and of Iago lead into an increasing complex of issues difficult to solve; the very simple fact of Othello's moral stature, and the value we assign to it, is anything but simple. Can Othello be in any way heroic—as distinct from central—when he is so deceived, deranged to the point of murder? On the other hand, the *way* in which Othello came to be deceived and the steps toward his derangement are strikingly clear—unmistakably so.

The plot, then, can be recollected simply and this simplicity is both necessary and deliberate. Why it has to be so has already been suggested and will be explored later; put briefly, the plot must be easy enough to carry other difficulties, ones of emotion or character or moral dilemma. That it is dramatically and not just accidentally simple is of course what saves it from Cinthio. Consider the plot. The number of participants in the action is severely limited; of the small cast even fewer are important in function or meaning. What goes on has nothing to distract from itself. Doubly so, for there are no byways for the story to wander off into, nor are there larger areas for the characters to move in. Othello leaves off being general—as far as the play's story counts—from the moment of his landing on Cyprus; he is always the imagined injured husband. It is not a State that is threatened, not even its glory, but a marriage and a reputation. The emotions in question are not ambition for a throne, not revenge for a crime, but insane jealousy and vicious malice. Both the context of the drama and its energies are what could be called domestic, and are thus immediately painful. The relentless exposition of these is almost a drawn-out analysis of such pain. The question, of course, arises as to what it is that is being exposed, beyond the chain of events itself. And the difficulty begins even with the simplicities of the plot. The plot is very simple but it is also very much Iago's.

THE RELATIONSHIPS OF CHARACTER

What happens in the play, happens to Othello. He is undoubtedly central. But what happens to him is because of what Iago does. Iago feels himself injured, works out a way to avenge himself and get what he wants as well, and succeeds perhaps only too well—certainly as far as his desire to humiliate Othello. There are really two problems here, both closely connected. One is passivity, the other activity, or at least its cause. Can Othello be considered more than a victim, pathetic at the end when he is forcibly awakened from his nightmare? Can Iago's conduct be in any way accounted for, to explain the desolation he causes before he is finally exposed? Here the plot and its events present the problems, make a solution of some sort imperative, but will not provide a key on their own. It is the mind behind the act that must be discovered, to make sense of both the act and its consequences.

Iago's very deadly success in a way conceals him from us. All through the play he has been a master at manipulating appearances so that they seem to be an inescapable reality. Everyone about him—Othello, Desdemona, Cassio, and even his wife, Emilia—accept him as the standard of sanity and blunt common sense. He is always giving advice, acting helpfully, and above all, arranging and directing. The question that must be asked, absurd as it seems, is whether in fact he does succeed, on his own terms or anybody else's. The most immediate assumption arises on the strength of the play's close. Desdemona has been murdered and Othello ruined totally. That no sane motive could have led to such an overwhelming revenge will then encourage the dismissing of any motives. Iago is thus a genuine monster, a pathological villain, if one wishes for a psychological explanation, a diabolical one to a more philosophical interpreter: "a motiveless malignity" Coleridge chose to call the phenomenon.

Yet Iago has repeatedly offered clear grounds for his behavior and actions. His opening words establish the sense of injured merit he feels; to this, envy of the debonair Cassio and sexual suspicion of Othello are soon added. These are what prompt Iago to act; to what end he acts and how are just as important to link these beginnings with the tragic end. How Iago sets about his purposes is easily answered but less quickly demonstrated—the play is the demonstration. Similarly, his ends are there to be seen and yet the conclusion he achieves is not recovery of office but murder. What is important to remember is that Iago's villainy is both more and less than a case study or an ethical demonstration can reveal. He is more than simply pathic or impersonally diabolical, because he is human, if only in the gusto with which he drives his plot forward. If there is sickness here, it is of the more familiar kind a practical joker enjoys at the discomfiture of the victim of his joke. He is less than totally successful because practical jokes have a way of backfiring:

> Villain, be sure thou prove my love a whore,—
> Be sure of it; give me ocular proof;
> Or, by the worth of man's eternal soul,
> Thou hadst been better have been born a dog
> Than answer my waked wrath!

Iago's success is the sort his character allows: it is that of an inspired opportunism where every detail can be worked to his advantage. He forges his web of illusion from every stray happening, every casual word. His failure is also his character—his inability to place himself imaginatively in Othello's place. When Iago feels injured, he spins a clever plot; when Othello is confronted with what to him is an essential injury, he acts even if the action demanded must lead to murder and tragedy.

Othello's passivity, then, is also not as simple a matter as it would seem. Initially, it stands as a direct reflection of his trust; it corresponds to the loyalty he feels integral to his honor and his love. Emotionally, Othello is not so much being simply bewildered and blinded as co-operating with a trusted friend in the discovery of truth. It is Iago's skill to cripple this faith Othello has in friendship by isolating it from a world strange and scarcely known to the general:

> I know our country disposition well;
> In Venice they do let heaven see the pranks
> They dare not show their husbands; their best conscience
> Is—not to leave undone, but keep unknown.

Iago works on Othello's weaknesses—his social unease and his passionate temperament—to exploit them. In this, he succeeds to the point of driving Othello beyond civilized society and even beyond humanity. Othello's climax of fury, in its incoherence and the animality of its images, is literally insanity. But Othello recovers. He regains no insight into his marriage, for this Iago has destroyed as a falsely illusive ideal; he does, however, recapture, what he had before his marriage—a ruthless sense of justice that has served him as a personal standard all his years as a successful soldier. It is this soldier—a general punishing personal treachery—who kills Desdemona.

THE TRAGIC EFFECT

Othello helps the audience in an ambivalent way with the very problem that has been under discussion. He is his own first critic, giving us at the end of the play his own epitaph, one meant to provide not just an explanation of what he has done but of the very nature and meaning of this act. Consider the points Othello raises by way of proper explanation, the points *he* considers necessary to judge the final situation correctly. He demands only justice, but with it all its rigors and also all its illumination. This just light will show that Othello's weakness was not jealousy—not a tendency to suspicion but very much the extreme reverse. Othello committed himself all too well, and such a complete trust was for him the ironic threshold to blindness. The actual horror of his wife's murder is too close to him and has to be kept at the distance of a similitude, in the form of eloquent charade where Othello can act out both the self-betrayal and its just punishment:

> I took by th' throat the circumcised dog
> And smote him—thus.

Here, in his last formal address, Othello sums up both his roles, that of victim, "Like the base Indian," and that of avenger as he once was in Aleppo. He has come full circle; he is once more the decisive man of action and his last act is again, according to him, one of necessary justice, heroic and tragic at the same time.

What are we to make of Othello finally? To what extent can he be trusted now at the last when trust has been precisely his blind spot all through the play? One very direct answer is rather grim in its attitude to Othello, the man and the play—and that is that he is no more to be accepted now than he was earlier. In neither case, just before or just after the murder, are Othello's eyes open to truth; he continues to pursue shadows, pathetically, at the close, when the shadow he is trying to catch is that of his own former self, of the military heroism he tries to assume too late and too wrongly. T. S. Eliot has put his critical disenchantment with Othello's heroics very tellingly.

> I have always felt that I have never read a more terrible exposure of human weakness—of universal human weakness—than the last great speech of Othello . . . What Othello seems to me to be doing in making this speech is *cheering himself up*. He is endeavouring to escape reality, he has ceased to think about Desdemona, and is thinking about himself. Humility is the most difficult of all virtues to achieve; nothing dies harder than the desire to think well of oneself . . . He takes in the spectator, but the human motive is primarily to take in himself.
>
> (*Selected Essays*, 1951, p. 130) *

And yet humility somehow seems not quite what is wanted in the dramatic values set off by Othello's final words and situation. It is not a question of the value of humility but of its relevance in this context, a context that is a dramatic representation of a tragic and a heroic dilemma. Iago is the more fully understood (dramatically at any rate) if he is considered not so much of a devil; perhaps, similarly, Othello should have less saintliness expected of him. Rather than dismissing the recognition he finally achieves on the grounds of its psychological or moral thinness, let us consider what, in fact, it does amount to.

What it certainly does not offer is the solidity of reality that morally must be asked for in daily experience. One cannot throw off a murder with an apt anecdote or an old war story. But is it the familiar, the common-sensical reality we live in terms of, that should be brought to bear? If it is brought in as a measuring stick here, it can be easily used to beat up other parts of the play. For, after all, what is Othello punishing in his wife? He kills her for her adultery; her offense is against her marriage and her husband. And yet the play opens on the night of the marriage, and the voyage to Cyprus separates Cassio and Desdemona. Iago's accusations and insinuations occur almost immediately after. When could the crime have occurred, the specific one so important in Iago's accusations and Othello's jealousy? The problem can be perhaps put most simply in its theatrical terms. For Iago's plot to succeed, for it to be at all credible, it must be quick and unremitting; any encounter of all his dupes together, any corroboration with each other and his lies would be blatantly exposed. Then, too, Othello's passionate fury and his murderous determination must also be swift and concentrated to be authentic. As has been said, the bulk of the play is a tightly knit unit, mounting in tension, closed in almost

* This has been expressed even more belligerently: "Othello, for those who don't join in the traditional sentimentalization of the play, is a very obvious case. The essential point that has to be made is that his valedictory *coup de théâtre* represents a rhetorical inflation, a headily emotional glorification, of an incapacity for tragic experience that marks the ordinary moments of us all." F. R. Leavis, *The Common Pursuit*, 1962, p. 128.

claustrophobically by the island and the night. But against this concentration is set another perspective of time—a more leisurely and repetitive time when Iago has suspected or discovered Cassio's guilt. There are repeated references in the play that create an impression of the possibility of adultery. There is an undeviating pursuit of quick events to their inevitable end. Which of the two is right for the play's meaning? Logically one cancels out the other—there cannot be singleness and repetition, tension and leisure. But it is not temporal logic that is in question—it is dramatic conviction. Desdemona is punished swiftly and remorselessly for an adultery that Othello has had convincingly presented to him.

Such a disparateness—a separation from the common-sensical to create a distinct but authentic dramatic reality—can be seen working on Othello, and the meaning he has. Any such meaning must be established in terms of the play itself and not externally. This is the final way in which *Othello*, despite the painful nature of its subject and the madness, malice, and cruelty it presents so familiarly domesticated, is classical; the play is supremely self-consistent, self-sustaining. Othello has come full circle by the play's end, to achieve command once more, even at the price of ceasing "to think about Desdemona." It is this achievement that makes his presence heroic. To consider it tragic as well, one can note the discrepancy, almost an unavoidable discrepancy, between the heroic and the reality established by the whole understanding (including common sense along with imagination). Even further, one can accept such a separation and find the tragic quality, perhaps as Othello does himself, in the ability to look at it sufficiently to master it. In this way, *Othello* has sufficient kinship with Sophocles' *Oedipus* to deserve a classical stature.

STUDY QUESTIONS—*Othello*

ACT I

1. What purpose is served by postponing the introduction of Othello until the second scene? What do we learn of Iago's character, attitudes, and abilities in the first scene? What is told us of Othello's? How are these modified in the rest of the act?
2. What impression is created of Othello on his first appearance?
3. What is the basis of their love and marriage as Desdemona and Othello account for it? What would you suggest as the relative strengths and weaknesses likely in such a relationship?
4. Why does Iago use prose to express himself and to persuade Roderigo in Scene iii? Give in your own words the doctrine Iago develops to justify his behavior so as to encourage Roderigo.
5. What are Iago's motives (as he gives them in the closing lines of the act) for what he is to do? Do they seem adequate to you? If not, suggest some more convincing reasons for his line of behavior.
6. What is Iago intending to do?
7. What relation does this act have to the rest of the drama structurally?

ACT II

1. What dramatic benefits are achieved by disposing of the Turkish threat immediately?

2. Demonstrate how Cassio, Iago, and Othello each create a distinct impression of character and attitude in the language they use at meeting Desdemona. How accurate is each of these characterizations for the man involved?

3. What further motives does Iago introduce for his revenge? Assess the weight of these and their credibility.

4. What further insight is given us into Iago and Othello in the episode of Cassio's drunkenness and dismissal?

ACT III

1. Describe as accurately as you can the steps by which Iago creates suspicion in Othello's mind. What are the means (the rhetorical technique) he uses to reinforce his hints and insinuations?

2. What are the weaknesses in Othello that Iago recognizes and works upon in spinning his web of suggestions?

3. What previous steps had Iago taken to insure the greater success of his plot?

4. At what point does the crisis (the onset of jealousy in Othello) occur? Discuss the dramatic and the psychological conventions being made use of here.

5. At what point does the development of the jealousy take on a radically distinct nature? What is Iago's reaction—and how will this force him to alter what he has presumably intended? Consider the closing lines of Act III, Scene iii in this respect.

6. Describe carefully the dramatic change that occurs in Othello in terms of his behavior and the words and images he uses to express this change. Compare the imagery and language used by Iago in this context.

7. Describe Desdemona's reaction to this change in Othello, the effect on her and her explanation of it.

8. Discuss the importance of the lost handkerchief to
   - a) Iago's plot
   - b) Othello's behavior
   - c) Cassio's reaction.

ACT IV

1. Discuss Othello's "trance" in terms of
   - a) its dramatic function
   - b) the preparation for it by Iago
   - c) the results of it on Othello.

2. Describe in careful detail how Iago achieves his final persuasion of Othello.

3. What is the dramatic effect and consequence of the arrival in Cyprus of the Venetian legation?

4. Compare the ways in which Othello expresses himself to Desdemona (Act IV, Scene ii) with his exchanges with Iago and with his trance (Act IV, Scene i) in terms of the language, imagery, and rhythms used and the differing effects of these.

5. Compare Iago's manipulation of Roderigo to incite him to murder with his persuading of Othello to murder his wife earlier in the act. On the basis of this comparison, what conclusions can be drawn about Othello, Roderigo, and Iago?

6. By comparing the attitudes and behavior of Emilia and Desdemona in the last scene, what dramatic characterizations of each woman emerge? To what extent and how is Desdemona's character contributory to the success of Iago's plot?

ACT V

1. At what point does Iago's plot begin to collapse? How does Iago attempt to survive this miscarriage of his schemes?

2. How does Othello attempt to steel himself for his task and even to justify its necessity?

3. What is the exact point of Desdemona's admission of guilt for Othello? Describe the dramatic irony of this "confession" so as to reveal fully the ambiguity in it and Othello's prejudgment.

4. Describe in careful detail the discovery by Othello of the plot worked against him. To what point does Iago attempt to defend and save himself? What is Iago's final course of conduct and how would you account for this dramatically and/or psychologically?

5. Examine Othello's final address carefully, so as to consider the following:

a) the dramatic and psychological purpose and effect of this speech;
b) its linkages or contrasts (in rhythm and imagery and heroic attitudes) with any of Othello's previous addresses (consider particularly I, iii and IV, ii);
c) its accuracy as a summary of what has happened in the drama;
d) the evidence it provides for the nature of Othello's tragedy, for our assessment of him and of his fate.

GENERAL

1. Briefly summarize the tragic action of the play. What is unusual about the relative roles of Iago (the antagonist) and Othello (the hero) in terms of the plot? What influence does this have on the nature of the tragic effect of the play?

2. Enumerate what you consider to be the elements in *Othello* peculiar to it to make it distinct from any other of Shakespeare's plays. Consider the effects of these elements on the dramatic, thematic, and emotional structure of the play.

3. Discuss some of the significant effects of Elizabethan theatrical conventions and techniques such as:
   a) the use of time (the double time problem)
   b) the crisis psychology (Othello's attack of jealousy and his trance)
   c) the rhetorical set-piece (Othello's last address)
   d) the apron stage with its lack of scenery and distancing
   e) the Elizabethan attitude to the exotic (Italy, Cyprus, and the Moor).

4. Trace through some of the dominant imagery in the play, particularly that occurring in the speeches of the major characters. Describe its several functions such as:
   a) characterization
   b) localization
   c) choric comment on the action and its tragic effects.

Describe Othello's role in the drama in terms of his imagery and its changes.

5. If the synopsis of the play, baldly summarized, gives a certain inescapably painful and even sordid effect, how does Shakespeare save *Othello* from being a dramatized version of an Elizabethan police case? To what extent are the painful elements required for the total effect, and for the tragic effect intended?

6. What do each of the following passages indicate to us about the occasion, the speaker, and the dramatic development of the play:
   a) Keep up your bright swords, for the dew will rust them.
   b) O, beware, my lord, of jealousy!
      It is the green-eyed monster, which doth mock
      The meat it feeds on.
   c) Villain, be sure thou prove my love a whore!
      Be sure of it; give me the ocular proof . . .
   d) Why, we have galls; and though we have some grace,
      Yet have we some revenge. Let husbands know
      Their wives have sense like them.
   e) What shall I do to win my lord again?
      Good friend, go to him; for, by this light of heaven,
      I know not how I lost him.
   f) Speak of me as I am; nothing extenuate,
      Nor set down aught in malice.

Suggestions for Further Reading

A. C. Bradley, *Shakespearean Tragedy* (1904)
G. Wilson Knight, *The Wheel of Fire* (1930)
Robert B. Heilman, *Magic in the Web* (1956)
F. R. Leavis, *The Common Pursuit* (1952)
J. Dover Wilson, *The Essential Shakespeare* (1930)
G. Sanders, *A Shakespeare Primer* (1945)

OTHELLO, THE MOOR OF VENICE

DRAMATIS PERSONAE

DUKE OF VENICE.
BRABANTIO, *a senator.*
OTHER SENATORS.
GRATIANO, *brother to Brabantio.*
LODOVICO, *kinsman to Brabantio.*
OTHELLO, *a noble Moor in the service of the Venetian state.*
CASSIO, *his lieutenant.*
IAGO, *his ancient.*
RODERIGO, *a Venetian gentleman.*
MONTANO, *Othello's predecessor in the government of Cyprus.*
CLOWN, *servant to Othello.*

DESDEMONA, *daughter to Brabantio and wife to Othello.*
EMILIA, *wife to Iago.*
BIANCA, *mistress to Cassio.*

SAILOR, MESSENGER, HERALD, OFFICERS, GENTLEMEN, MUSICIANS, *and* ATTENDANTS.

SCENE—*Venice: a seaport in Cyprus.*

Othello

ACT I

ACT I

IAGO, a Venetian soldier, is intensely irritated that his commander, Othello, has promoted a Florentine, Michael Cassio, to a lieutenancy that Iago feels he deserves. He is out to get his own back, and this can be done most simply by breaking the news of Othello's elopement with Desdemona, a senator's daughter. Using a foolish former suitor, Roderigo, as his messenger, Iago rouses Brabantio, the father, to hunt down the newly wedded pair. Brabantio accuses Othello of having used sorcery to trap his daughter, for she is separated from Othello by years, upbringing, and race, and the match is, for Brabantio, unnatural. The general is desperately needed by the Venetian state, however, since he is about to be sent to defend Cyprus against the Turks, and Brabantio is left bitterly unsatisfied. Othello is to leave for Cyprus immediately and has Desdemona follow after with "honest" Iago. The act closes with Iago working out some more telling stroke that will get him the position he covets and at the same time humiliate Othello for the indignities and injuries Iago feels have been done him.

ACT I. SCENE I.

Venice. A street.

Enter RODERIGO *and* IAGO.

RODERIGO.

Tush, never tell me; I take it much unkindly
That thou, Iago, who hast had my purse
As if the strings were thine, shouldst know of this,—

IAGO.

'Sblood,[1] but you will not hear me:—
If ever I did dream of such a matter,
Abhor me.

RODERIGO.

Thou told'st me thou didst hold him in thy hate.

IAGO.

Despise me, if I do not. Three great ones of the city,
In personal suit to make me his lieutenant,
Off-capt to him[2]:—and, by the faith of man,
I know my price, I am worth no worse a place:—
But he, as loving his own pride and purposes,
Evades them, with a bombast circumstance
Horribly stuft with epithets of war;[3]

---

[1] **'Sblood:** God's blood (a mild oath).

[2] **Off-capt to him:** took their caps in hand, humbling themselves before him (Othello).

[3] **a bombast circumstance/Horribly stuft with epithets of war:** high-sounding words (meaning nothing) couched in military terms.

And, in conclusion,
Nonsuits[1] my mediators; for, 'Certes,' [2] says he,
'I have already chose my officer.'
And what was he?
Forsooth, a great arithmetician,[3]
One Michael Cassio, a Florentine,
A fellow almost damn'd in a fair wife;[4]
That never set a squadron in the field,
Nor the division of a battle knows
More than a spinster; unless the bookish theoric,[5]
Wherein the toged consuls can propose
As masterly as he: mere prattle, without practice,[6]
Is all his soldiership. But he, sir, had th'election:[7]
And I—of whom his eyes had seen the proof
At Rhodes, at Cyprus, and on other grounds
Christian and heathen—must be be-lee'd and calm'd [8]
By debitor and creditor; this counter-caster,[9]
He, in good time, must his lieutenant be,
And I—God bless the mark!—his Moorships' ancient.[10]

RODERIGO.

By heaven, I rather would have been his hangman.

IAGO.

Why, there's no remedy; 'tis the curse of service,
Preferment goes by letter and affection,
And not by old gradation, where each second
Stood heir to th' first. Now, sir, be judge yourself,
Whether I in any just term am affined [11]
To love the Moor.

RODERIGO.

I would not follow him, then.

---

[1] **Nonsuits:** denies the petition of. [2] **'Certes':** in truth. [3] **arithmetician:** a student of military tactics as explained in books. [4] **almost damn'd in a fair wife:** barely escaped marriage to a beautiful woman. [5] **theoric:** theoretics. [6] **without practice:** without experience. [7] **had th'election:** was elected. [8] **be-lee'd and calm'd:** Cassio has gotten in front of him and he cannot go on. [9] **counter-caster:** one who calculates with counters. [10] **ancient:** aide-de-camp. [11] **affined:** obligated.

IAGO.

O, sir, content you;
I follow him to serve my turn upon him:
We cannot all be masters, nor all masters
Cannot be truly follow'd. You shall mark
Many a duteous and knee-crooking[1] knave,
That, doting on his own obsequious bondage,
Wears out[2] his time, much like his master's ass,
For naught but provender; and, when he's old, cashier'd:
Whip me such honest knaves. Others there are,
Who, trimm'd in forms and visages of duty,[3]
Keep yet their hearts attending on themselves;
And, throwing but shows of service on their lords,
Do well thrive by them, and, when they have lined their coats,[4]
Do themselves homage:[5] these fellows have some soul;
And such a one do I profess myself.
For, sir,
It is as sure as you are Roderigo,
Were I the Moor, I would not be Iago:
In following him, I follow but myself;
Heaven is my judge, not I for love and duty,
But seeming so, for my peculiar end:
For when my outward action doth demonstrate
The native[6] act and figure of my heart
In compliment extern,[7] 'tis not long after
But I will wear my heart upon my sleeve
For daws[8] to peck at: I am not what I am.[9]

RODERIGO.

What a full fortune does the thick-lips owe,
If he can carry't thus!

---

[1] **knee-crooking:** bowing. [2] **Wears out:** serves. [3] **trimm'd in forms and visages of duty:** trained in the outward appearance of duty (service). [4] **coats:** i.e., pockets. [5] **Do themselves homage:** serve their own interests. [6] **native:** natural. [7] **compliment extern:** outward show of civility. [8] **daws:** jackdaws. [9] **I am not what I am:** I am not what I appear to be.

IAGO.

Call up her father,
Rouse him:—make after him, poison his delight,
Proclaim him in the streets; incense her kinsmen:
And though he in a fertile climate[1] dwell,
Plague him with flies,[2] though that his joy be joy,
Yet throw such changes of vexation on't,
As it may lose some colour.

RODERIGO.

Here is her father's house; I'll call aloud.

IAGO.

Do; with like timorous accent[3] and dire yell
As when, by night and negligence, the fire
Is spied in populous cities.

RODERIGO.

What, ho, Brabantio! Signior Brabantio, ho!

IAGO.

Awake! what, ho, Brabantio! thieves! thieves! thieves!
Look to your house, your daughter, and your bags!
Thieves! thieves!

BRABANTIO *appears above, at a window.*

BRABANTIO.

What is the reason of this terrible summons?
What is the matter there?

RODERIGO.

Signior, is all your family within?

IAGO.

Are your doors lockt?

BRABANTIO.

Why, wherefore ask you this?

IAGO.

Zounds,[4] sir, y'are robb'd; for shame, put on your gown;

---

[1] in a fertile climate: in a tranquil state of mind.
[2] flies: troubles; vexations.
[3] timorous accent: terrified voice.
[4] Zounds: God's wounds (a mild oath).

Your heart is burst, you have lost half your soul;
Even now, now, very now, an old black ram
Is tupping[1] your white ewe. Arise, arise;
Awake the snorting[2] citizens with the bell,
Or else the devil will make a grandsire of you:
Arise, I say.

BRABANTIO.

What, have you lost your wits?

RODERIGO.

Most reverend signior, do you know my voice?

BRABANTIO.

Not I: what are you?

RODERIGO.

My name is Roderigo.

BRABANTIO.

The worser welcome:
I have charged thee not to haunt about my doors:
In honest plainness thou hast heard me say
My daughter is not for thee; and now, in madness,
Being full of supper and distempering draughts,[3]
Upon malicious bravery, dost thou come
To start[4] my quiet;—

RODERIGO.

Sir, sir, sir,—

BRABANTIO.

But thou must needs be sure
My spirit and my place have in them power
To make this bitter[5] to thee.

RODERIGO.

Patience, good sir.

---

[1] **tupping:** covering.
[2] **snorting:** snoring.
[3] **distempering draughts:** intoxicating drinks.
[4] **start:** disturb.
[5] **bitter:** unpleasant.

BRABANTIO.

What tell'st thou me of robbing? this is Venice;
My house is not a grange.[1]

RODERIGO.

Most grave Brabantio,
In simple and pure soul I come to you.

IAGO.

Zounds, sir, you are one of those that will not serve God, if the devil bid you. Because we come to do you service, and you think we are ruffians, you'll have your daughter cover'd with a Barbary horse; you'll have your nephews[2] neigh to you; you'll have coursers for cousins, and gennets[3] for germans.[4]

BRABANTIO.

What profane wretch art thou?

IAGO.

I am one, sir, that comes to tell you your daughter and the Moor are now making the beast with two backs.

BRABANTIO.

Thou art a villain.

IAGO.

You are—a senator.

BRABANTIO.

This thou shalt answer: I know thee, Roderigo.

RODERIGO.

Sir, I will answer any thing. But, I beseech you,
If't be your pleasure and most wise consent,
As partly I find it is, that your fair daughter,
At this odd-even[5] and dull watch o'the night,
Transported, with no worse nor better guard
But with a knave of common hire, a gondolier,

---

[1] **grange:** an isolated house or farmhouse.
[2] **nephews:** lineal descendants.
[3] **gennets:** small Spanish horses.
[4] **germans:** close blood relatives.
[5] **odd-even:** an indeterminate time between midnight and daybreak.

To the gross clasps of a lascivious Moor,—
If this be known to you, and your allowance,[1]
We then have done you bold and saucy wrongs;
But, if you know not this, my manners tell me
We have your wrong[2] rebuke. Do not believe
That, from the sense of all civility,
I thus would play and trifle with your reverence:
Your daughter,—if you have not given her leave,—
I say again, hath made a gross[3] revolt;
Tying her duty, beauty, wit, and fortunes,
In an extravagant and wheeling[4] stranger
Of here and every where. Straight[5] satisfy yourself:
If she be in her chamber or your house,
Let loose on me the justice of the state
For thus deluding you.

BRABANTIO.

Strike on the tinder, ho!
Give me a taper!—call up all my people!—
This accident is not unlike my dream:
Belief of it oppresses me already.—
Light, I say! light! [*Exit above.*

IAGO.

Farewell; for I must leave you:
It seems not meet,[6] nor wholesome to my place,[7]
To be produced—as, if I stay, I shall—
Against the Moor: for, I do know, the state,
However this may gall him with some check,[8]
Cannot with safety cast[9] him; for he's embarkt
With such loud [10] reason to the Cyprus wars,
Which even now stand in act, that, for their souls,
Another of his fadom[11] they have none
To lead their business: in which regard,

---

[1] **your allowance:** with your permission. [2] **wrong:** undeserved. [3] **gross:** flagrantly obvious. [4] **extravagant and wheeling:** wandering and homeless (a soldier of fortune). [5] **Straight:** immediately. [6] **meet:** suitable; proper. [7] **place:** position; rank. [8] **some check:** some rebuke. [9] **cast:** dismiss. [10] **loud:** important. [11] **fadom:** judgment; capability.

Though I do hate him as I do hell-pains,
Yet, for necessity of present life,
I must show out a flag and sign of love,
Which is indeed but sign. That you shall surely find him,
Lead to the Sagittary[1] the raised search;[2]
And there will I be with him. So, farewell. [*Exit.*

Enter, below, BRABANTIO, *with* SERVANTS *and torches.*

BRABANTIO.
It is too true an evil: gone she is;
And what's to come of my despised time[3]
Is naught but bitterness.—Now, Roderigo,
Where didst thou see her?—O unhappy girl!—.
With the Moor, say'st thou?—Who would be a father!—
How didst thou know 'twas she?—O, she deceives me
Past thought!—What said she to you?—Get more tapers;
Raise all my kindred.—Are they married, think you?

RODERIGO.
Truly, I think they are.

BRABANTIO.
O heaven!—How got she out?—O treason of the blood!—
Fathers, from hence trust not your daughters' minds
By what you see them act.—Is there not charms
By which the property[4] of youth and maidhood
May be abused?[5] Have you not read, Roderigo,
Of some such thing?

---

[1] **Sagittary:** the Sign of the Sagittary (the archer)—generally supposed to have been an inn. [2] **raised search:** the men pressed into service to aid in the search. [3] **my despised time:** the remaining years of my life. [4] **property:** faculties; nature. [5] **abused:** made subject to illusions; that is, deluded.

RODERIGO.

Yes, sir, I have indeed.

BRABANTIO.

Call up my brother.—O, would you had had her!—
Some one way, some another.—Do you know
Where we may apprehend her and the Moor?

RODERIGO.

I think I can discover him, if you please
To get good guard, and go along with me.

BRABANTIO.

Pray you, lead on. At every house I'll call;
I may command at most.[1]—Get weapons, ho!
And raise some special officers of night.[2]—
On, good Roderigo;—I'll deserve[3] your pains. [*Exeunt.*

SCENE II.

Another street.

Enter OTHELLO, IAGO, *and* ATTENDANTS *with torches.*

IAGO.

Though in the trade of war I have slain men,
Yet do I hold it very stuff [4] o'the conscience
To do no contrived murder: I lack iniquity
Sometimes to do me service: nine or ten times
I had thought t'have yerkt[5] him here under the ribs.

OTHELLO.

'Tis better as it is.

IAGO.

Nay, but he prated,
And spoke such scurvy[6] and provoking terms

---

[1] **command at most:** have influence at most of them.
[2] **some special officers of night:** the night watch.
[3] **deserve:** reward.
[4] **stuff:** essence; substance.
[5] **yerkt:** hit smartly; jabbed.
[6] **scurvy:** low; contemptible.

Against your honour,
That, with the little godliness I have,
I did full hard forbear him. But, I pray you, sir,
Are you fast[1] married? Be assured of this,
That the magnifico[2] is much beloved;
And hath, in his effect, a voice potential
As double as the duke's:[3] he will divorce you;
Or put upon you what restraint and grievance
The law—with all his might t'enforce it on—
Will give him cable.[4]

OTHELLO.

Let him do his spite:
My services which I have done the signiory[5]
Shall out-tongue his complaints. 'Tis yet[6] to know,—
Which, when I know that boasting is an honour,
I shall promulgate,—I fetch my life and being
From men of royal siege;[7] and my demerits[8]
May speak, unbonneted,[9] to as proud a fortune
As this that I have reacht:[10] for know, Iago,
But that I love the gentle Desdemona,
I would not my unhoused [11] free condition
Put into circumscription and confine
For the sea's worth. But, look! what lights come yond?

IAGO.

Those are the raised father and his friends:
You were best go in.

OTHELLO.

Not I; I must be found:
My parts, my title, and my perfect soul [12]
Shall manifest me rightly. Is it they?

---

[1] **fast:** securely; legally. [2] **magnifico:** Brabantio. [3] **a voice . . . duke's:** influence as great as the duke's, whose office gives him double powers. [4] **cable:** rope; range. [5] **signiory:** the Venetian government. [6] **yet:** as yet. [7] **men of royal siege:** i.e., kings. [8] **demerits:** merits. [9] **unbonneted:** openly. [10] **reacht:** that is, married into. [11] **unhoused:** unmarried. [12] **perfect soul:** clear conscience.

IAGO.
By Janus,[1] I think no.

Enter CASSIO, *and certain* OFFICERS *with torches.*

OTHELLO.
The servants of the duke, and my lieutenant.—
The goodness of the night upon you, friends!
What is the news?

CASSIO.
The duke does greet you, general
And he requires your haste-post-haste[2] appearance
Even on the instant.

OTHELLO.
What is the matter, think you?

CASSIO.
Something from Cyprus, as I may divine:
It is a business of some heat:[3] the galleys
Have sent a dozen sequent[4] messengers
This very night at one another's heels;
And many of the consuls, raised and met,
Are at the duke's already: you have been hotly call'd for;
When, being not at your lodging to be found,
The senate hath sent about three several [5] quests
To search you out.

OTHELLO.
'Tis well I am found by you.
I will but spend a word here in the house,
And go with you. [*Exit.*

CASSIO.
Ancient, what makes he here?

IAGO.
Faith, he to-night hath boarded a land carack:[6]
If it prove lawful prize, he's made for ever.

---

[1] **Janus:** the double-faced Roman deity. [2] **haste-post-haste:** these words were written on packets or letters to insure speedy delivery. [3] **heat:** urgency. [4] **sequent:** following one after the other. [5] **several:** separate. [6] **carack:** a ship capable of carrying a large cargo, like a Spanish galleon.

CASSIO.
I do not understand.

IAGO.
He's married.

CASSIO.
To who?

Enter OTHELLO.

IAGO.
Marry, to—Come, captain, will you go?

OTHELLO.
Have with you.[1]

CASSIO.
Here comes another troop to seek for you.

IAGO.
It is Brabantio:—general, be advised;[2]
He comes to bad intent.[3]

Enter BRABANTIO, RODERIGO, *and* OFFICERS *with torches and weapons.*

OTHELLO.
Holla! stand there!

RODERIGO.
Signior, it is the Moor.

BRABANTIO.
Down with him, thief!
[*They draw on both sides.*

IAGO.
You, Roderigo! come, sir, I am for you.

OTHELLO.
Keep up your bright swords, for the dew will rust them.—
Good signior, you shall more command with years
Than with your weapons.[4]

---

[1] Have with you: I'm with you.
[2] be advised: be cautious.
[3] to bad intent: with bad intentions.
[4] you shall more command with years/Than with your weapons: that is, your age commands more respect than do your weapons.

BRABANTIO.

O thou foul thief, where hast thou stow'd my daughter?
Damn'd as thou art, thou hast enchanted her;
For I'll refer me to[1] all things of sense,
If she in chains of magic were not bound,
Whether a maid so tender, fair, and happy,
So opposite[2] to marriage that she shunn'd
The wealthy curled darlings of our nation,
Would ever have, t'incur a general mock,[3]
Run from her guardage[4] to the sooty bosom
Of such a thing as thou,—to fear, not to delight.
Judge me the world,[5] if 'tis not gross in sense[6]
That thou hast practised on her with foul charms;
Abused her delicate youth with drugs or minerals
That weaken motion:[7]—I'll have't disputed on;
'Tis probable, and palpable to thinking.
I therefore apprehend and do attach[8] thee
For an abuser of the world, a practiser
Of arts[9] inhibited and out of warrant.[10]—
Lay hold upon him: if he do resist,
Subdue him at his peril.

OTHELLO.

Hold your hands,
Both you of my inclining, and the rest:
Were it my cue to fight, I should have known it
Without a prompter.—Where will you that I go
To answer this your charge?

BRABANTIO.

To prison; till fit time
Of law, and course of direct session,[11]
Call thee to answer.

---

[1] **refer me to:** appeal to. [2] **opposite:** opposed. [3] **general mock:** public shame or contempt. [4] **guardage:** guardianship. [5] **Judge me the world:** let the world judge me. [6] **gross in sense:** obvious. [7] **motion:** judgment; emotions. [8] **attach:** arrest. [9] **arts:** black magic. [10] **inhibited and out of warrant:** prohibited and illegal. [11] **course of direct session:** regular course of procedure.

OTHELLO.

What if I do obey?
How may the duke be therewith satisfied,
Whose messengers are here about my side,
Upon some present business[1] of the state
To bring me to him?

FIRST OFFICER.

'Tis true, most worthy signior;
The duke's in council, and your noble self,
I am sure, is sent for.

BRABANTIO.

How! the duke in council!
In this time of the night!—Bring him away;
Mine's not an idle cause: the duke himself,
Or any of my brothers of the state,
Cannot but feel this wrong as 'twere their own;
For if such actions may have passage free,
Bond-slaves and pagans shall our statesmen be.

[*Exeunt.*

SCENE III.

A council-chamber.

The DUKE *and* SENATORS *sitting at a table;* OFFICERS *attending.*

DUKE.

There is no composition[2] in these news[3]
That gives them credit.[4]

FIRST SENATOR.

Indeed, they are disproportion'd;
My letters say a hundred and seven galleys.

DUKE.

And mine, a hundred and forty.

SECOND SENATOR.

And mine, two hundred:

---

[1] present business: that is, business now in the process of being transacted.
[2] composition: consistency.
[3] these news: these tidings.
[4] credit: credibility.

But though they jump[1] not on a just account,—
As in these cases, where the aim[2] reports,
'Tis oft with difference,—yet do they all confirm
A Turkish fleet, and bearing up to Cyprus.

DUKE.
Nay, it is possible enough to judgement:
I do not so secure me in the error,[3]
But the main article[4] I do approve[5]
In fearful sense.

SAILOR [*within*].
What, ho! what, ho! what, ho!

FIRST OFFICER.
A messenger from the galleys.

Enter a SAILOR.

DUKE.
Now, what's the business?

SAILOR.
The Turkish preparation makes for Rhodes;
So was I bid report here to the state
By Signior Angelo.

DUKE.
How say you by this change?

FIRST SENATOR.
This cannot be,
By no assay of reason:[6] 'tis a pageant,[7]
To keep us in false gaze.[8] When we consider
Th'importancy of Cyprus to the Turk;
And let ourselves again but understand,
That as it more concerns the Turk than Rhodes,
So may he with more facile question[9] bear it,
For that it stands not in such warlike brace,[10]

---

[1] **jump:** agree. [2] **the aim:** that is, no better ground for information than conjecture. [3] **I . . . error:** I do not feel overconfident about the discrepancy. [4] **main article:** i.e., the fact that the fleet is approaching. [5] **approve:** acknowledge. [6] **assay of reason:** test of reasoning. [7] **pageant:** show. [8] **in false gaze:** our attention diverted. [9] **more facile question:** an easier struggle. [10] **brace:** readiness.

But altogether lacks th'abilities
That Rhodes is drest in:—if we make thought of this,
We must not think the Turk is so unskilful
To leave that latest[1] which concerns him first,
Neglecting an attempt of ease and gain,
To wake and wage a danger profitless.

DUKE.
Nay, in all confidence, he's not for Rhodes.

FIRST OFFICER.
Here is more news.

Enter a MESSENGER.

MESSENGER.
The Ottomites,[2] reverend and gracious,
Steering with due course toward the isle of Rhodes,
Have there injointed [3] them with an after fleet.[4]

FIRST SENATOR.
Ay, so I thought. How many, as you guess?

MESSENGER.
Of thirty sail: and now they do re-stem
Their backward course,[5] bearing with frank appearance
Their purposes toward Cyprus.—Signior Montano,
Your trusty and most valiant servitor,
With his free duty[6] recommends[7] you thus,
And prays you to believe him.

DUKE.
'Tis certain, then, for Cyprus.—
Marcus Luccicos, is not he in town?

FIRST SENATOR.
He's now in Florence.

---

[1] **latest:** till the last. [2] **Ottomites:** the Turks. [3] **injointed:** joined. [4] **after fleet:** fleet following them. [5] **re-stem/Their backward course:** turn in the opposite direction from their former course. [6] **his free duty:** his unlimited respect. [7] **recommends:** informs.

DUKE.
Write from us to him; post-post-haste dispatch.

FIRST SENATOR.
Here comes Brabantio and the valiant Moor.

Enter BRABANTIO, OTHELLO, IAGO, RODERIGO, *and* OFFICERS.

DUKE.
Valiant Othello, we must straight employ you
Against the general enemy Ottoman.—
[*to* BRABANTIO] I did not see you; welcome, gentle signior;
We lackt[1] your counsel and your help to-night.

BRABANTIO.
So did I yours. Good your Grace,[2] pardon me;
Neither my place, nor aught I heard of business,
Hath raised me from my bed; nor doth the general care
Take hold on me; for my particular grief
Is of so flood-gate and o'erbearing nature
That it engluts[3] and swallows other sorrows,
And it is still itself.

DUKE.
Why, what's the matter?

BRABANTIO.
My daughter! O, my daughter!

DUKE *and* SENATOR.
Dead?

BRABANTIO.
Ay, to me;
She is abused, stoln from me, and corrupted
By spells and medicines bought of mountebanks;[4]
For nature so preposterously to err,
Being not deficient, blind, or lame of sense,
Sans[5] witchcraft could not.

---

[1] **lackt:** missed.
[2] **Good your Grace:** your good Grace.
[3] **engluts:** engulfs; swallows.
[4] **mountebanks:** literally, one who mounts a bench or platform in a park or carnival and sells quack medicine; unscrupulous pretender.
[5] **Sans:** without.

DUKE.

Whoe'er he be that, in this foul proceeding,
Hath thus beguiled your daughter of herself,
And you of her, the bloody book of law
You shall yourself read in the bitter letter
After your own sense;[1] yea, though our proper son
Stood in your action.[2]

BRABANTIO.

Humbly I thank your Grace.
Here is the man, this Moor; whom now, it seems,
Your special mandate, for the state-affairs,
Hath hither brought.

DUKE *and* SENATOR.

We are very sorry for't.

DUKE [*to* OTHELLO].

What, in your own part, can you say to this?

BRABANTIO.

Nothing, but this is so.

OTHELLO.

Most potent, grave, and reverend signiors,
My very noble and approved [3] good masters,
That I have ta'en away this old man's daughter,
It is most true; true, I have married her:
The very head and front of my offending
Hath this extent, no more. Rude am I in my speech,
And little blest with the soft phrase of peace;
For since these arms of mine had seven years' pith,[4]
Till now some nine moons wasted,[5] they have used
Their dearest[6] action in the tented field;[7]
And little of this great world can I speak,
More than pertains to feats of broil and battle;
And therefore little shall I grace my cause

---

[1] **After your own sense:** according to your own interpretation. [2] **though our proper son/Stood in your action:** even though our own son were answering your charges. [3] **approved:** tested; proved. [4] **pith:** strength; muscle. [5] **Till now some nine moons wasted:** until nine months ago. [6] **dearest:** most important. [7] **tented field:** camps of war.

In speaking for myself. Yet, by your gracious patience,
I will a round [1] unvarnisht tale deliver
Of my whole course of love; what drugs, what charms,
What conjuration, and what mighty magic,—
For such proceeding I am charged withal,—
I won his daughter.

BRABANTIO.

A maiden never bold;
Of spirit so still and quiet, that her motion[2]
Blusht at herself; and she—in spite of nature,
Of years, of country, credit, every thing—
To fall in love with what she fear'd to look on!
It is a judgement maim'd and most imperfect,
That will confess perfection so could err
Against all rules of nature; and must be driven
To find out practices[3] of cunning hell,
Why this should be. I therefore vouch again,
That with some mixtures powerful o'er the blood,
Or with some dram conjured to this effect,
He wrought upon her.

DUKE.

To vouch this, is no proof,
Without more wider and more overt test
Than these thin habits[4] and poor likelihoods
Of modern[5] seeming do prefer against him.

FIRST SENATOR.

But, Othello, speak:
Did you by indirect and forced [6] courses
Subdue and poison this young maid's affections?
Or came it by request, and such fair question[7]
As soul to soul affordeth?

---

[1] **round:** blunt; plain. [2] **motion:** natural inclination; impulse. [3] **practices:** treacherous stratagems. [4] **thin habits:** flimsy trappings. [5] **modern:** commonplace; trivial. [6] **indirect and forced:** deceitful and unnatural. [7] **question:** discourse.

OTHELLO.

I do beseech you,
Send for the lady to the Sagittary,
And let her speak of me before her father:
If you do find me foul in her report,
The trust, the office, I do hold of you,
Not only take away, but let your sentence
Even fall upon my life.

DUKE.

Fetch Desdemona hither.

OTHELLO.

Ancient, conduct them, you best know the place.—

[*Exeunt* IAGO *and* ATTENDANTS.

And, till she come, as truly as to heaven
I do confess the vices of my blood,
So justly[1] to your grave ears I'll present
How I did thrive in this fair lady's love,
And she in mine.

DUKE.

Say it, Othello.

OTHELLO.

Her father loved me; oft invited me;
Still [2] question'd me the story of my life,
From year to year,—the battles, sieges, fortunes,
That I have past.
I ran it through, even from my boyish days
To the very moment that he bade me tell it:
Wherein I spake of most disastrous chances,[3]
Of moving[4] accidents by flood and field;
Of hair-breadth scapes i'th'imminent[5] deadly breach;
Of being taken by the insolent foe,
And sold to slavery; of my redemption thence,

---

[1] **justly:** truthfully.
[2] **Still:** constantly.
[3] **chances:** incidents of battle—the chances he took.
[4] **moving:** exciting.
[5] **imminent:** threatening.

And portance[1] in my travel's history:
Wherein of antres vast and deserts idle,[2]
Rough quarries, rocks, and hills whose heads touch heaven,
It was my hint[3] to speak,—such was the process;
And of the Cannibals that each other eat,
The Anthropophagi,[4] and men whose heads
Do grow beneath their shoulders. This to hear
Would Desdemona seriously incline:
But still the house-affairs would draw her thence;
Which ever as she could with haste dispatch,
She'ld come again, and with a greedy ear
Devour up my discourse:—which I observing,
Took once a pliant[5] hour; and found good means
To draw from her a prayer of earnest heart
That I would all my pilgrimage dilate,[6]
Whereof by parcels she had something heard,
But not intentively:[7] I did consent;
And often did beguile her of her tears,
When I did speak of some distressful stroke
That my youth suffer'd. My story being done,
She gave me for my pains a world of sighs:
She swore,—in faith, 'twas strange, 'twas passing[8] strange;
'Twas pitiful, 'twas wondrous pitiful:
She wisht she had not heard it: yet she wisht
That heaven had made her such a man: she thankt me;
And bade me, if I had a friend that loved her,
I should but teach him how to tell my story,
And that would woo her. Upon this hint[9] I spake:
She loved me for the dangers I had past;
And I loved her that she did pity them.

---

[1] **portance:** my behavior; bearing or deportment. [2] **antres vast and deserts idle:** vast caves or grottoes, and trackless wastes. [3] **hint:** occasion. [4] **Anthropophagi:** from Greek word meaning "the eating of men"; cannibals. [5] **pliant:** yielding; advantageous. [6] **dilate:** relate at length. [7] **intentively:** consecutively, or as a whole; in detail. [8] **passing:** surpassingly. [9] **hint:** cue.

This only is the witchcraft I have used:—
Here comes the lady; let her witness it.

Enter DESDEMONA *with* IAGO *and* ATTENDANTS.

DUKE.

I think this tale would win my daughter too.—
Good Brabantio,
Take up this mangled matter at the best:[1]
Men do their broken weapons rather use
Than their bare hands.[2]

BRABANTIO.

I pray you, hear her speak:
If she confess that she was half the wooer,
Destruction on my head, if my bad [3] blame
Light on the man!—Come hither, gentle mistress:
Do you perceive in all this noble company
Where most you owe obedience?

DESDEMONA.

My noble father,
I do perceive here a divided duty:
To you I am bound [4] for life and education;
My life and education both do learn[5] me
How to respect you; you are the lord of duty,—
I am hitherto your daughter: but here's my husband;
And so much duty as my mother show'd
To you, preferring you before her father,
So much I challenge that I may profess
Due to the Moor my lord.

BRABANTIO.

God be wi' you! I have done.
Please it your Grace, on to the state-affairs:
I had rather to adopt a child than get[6] it.—

---

[1] **Take up this mangled matter at the best:** try to make the best of this sorry business. [2] **Men do their broken weapons rather use/Than their bare hands:** It is better for men to try to patch up differences rather than to use violence. [3] **bad:** unjust. [4] **bound:** obligated. [5] **learn:** teach. [6] **get:** beget.

Come hither, Moor:
I here do give thee that with all my heart
Which, but thou hast already, with all my heart
I would keep from thee.—For your sake,[1] jewel,
I am glad at soul I have no other child;
For thy escape would teach me tyranny,
To hang clogs on them.[2]—I have done, my lord.

DUKE.

Let me speak like yourself;[3] and lay a sentence,
Which, as a grise[4] or step, may help these lovers
Into your favour.
When remedies are past, the griefs are ended
By seeing the worst, which late on hopes depended.
To mourn a mischief that is past and gone
Is the next way to draw new mischief on.
What cannot be preserved when fortune takes,
Patience her injury a mockery makes.
The robb'd that smiles steals something from the thief;
He robs himself that spends a bootless[5] grief.

BRABANTIO.

So let the Turk of Cyprus us beguile;
We lose it not, so long as we can smile.
He bears the sentence well that nothing bears
But the free comfort[6] which from thence he hears;
But he bears both the sentence and the sorrow
That to pay grief must of poor patience borrow.
These sentences, to sugar, or to gall,
Being strong on both sides, are equivocal:[7]
But words are words; I never yet did hear
That the bruised heart was pierced through the ear.—

---

[1] **For your sake:** because of you. [2] **To hang clogs on them:** that is, to put them in hanging clogs (clogs were weights used to hamper movement). [3] **like yourself:** i.e., as you would speak if you were in a more rational mood. [4] **a grise:** a step. [5] **bootless:** useless; valueless. [6] **free comfort:** the consolation of free moral advice. [7] **equivocal:** equal.

I humbly beseech you, proceed to th'affairs of state.

DUKE.

The Turk with a most mighty preparation makes for Cyprus: —Othello, the fortitude[1] of the place is best known to you; and though we have there a substitute[2] of most allow'd sufficiency,[3] yet opinion, a sovereign mistress of effects,[4] throws a more safer voice on you:[5] you must therefore be content to slubber the gloss[6] of your new fortunes with this more stubborn and boisterous[7] expedition.

OTHELLO.

The tyrant custom, most grave senators,
Hath made the flinty and steel couch of war
My thrice-driven[8] bed of down: I do agnize[9]
A natural and prompt alacrity
I find in hardness; and do undertake
This present war against the Ottomites.
Most humbly, therefore, bending to your state,
I crave fit disposition for my wife;
Due reference of place and exhibition;[10]
With such accommodation and besort[11]
As levels with[12] her breeding.

DUKE.

If you please,
Be't at her father's.

BRABANTIO.

I'll not have it so.

OTHELLO.

Nor I.

DESDEMONA.

Nor I; I would not there reside,
To put my father in impatient thoughts

---

[1] **fortitude:** fortifications; strength. [2] **substitute:** viceroy. [3] **most allow'd sufficiency:** acknowledged efficiency. [4] **effects:** results. [5] **throws . . . you:** selects you as the safest person for command. [6] **slubber the gloss:** obscure the radiance. [7] **stubborn and boisterous:** difficult and violent. [8] **Thrice-driven:** very soft. [9] **agnize:** acknowledge. [10] **exhibition:** allowance. [11] **besort:** escort. [12] **As levels with:** as is on a par with.

By being in his eye. Most gracious duke,
To my unfolding lend your prosperous ear;[1]
And let me find a charter[2] in your voice,
T'assist my simpleness.

DUKE.

What would you, Desdemona?

DESDEMONA.

That I did love the Moor to live with him,
My downright violence[3] and storm of fortunes
May trumpet to the world: my heart's subdued [4]
Even to the very quality[5] of my lord:
I saw Othello's visage in his mind;[6]
And to his honours and his valiant parts[7]
Did I my soul and fortunes consecrate.
So that, dear lords, if I be left behind,
A moth of peace, and he go to the war,
The rites for which I love him are bereft me,
And I a heavy[8] interim shall support
By his dear absence. Let me go with him.

OTHELLO.

Your voices,[9] lords: beseech you, let her will
Have a free way.
Vouch with me, heaven, I therefore beg it not,
To please the palate of my appetite;
Nor to comply with heat[10]—the young affects[11]
In me defunct—and proper satisfaction;
But to be free and bounteous to her mind:[12]
And heaven defend your good souls, that you think
I will your serious and great business scant[13]
For[14] she is with me: no, when light-wing'd toys
Of feather'd Cupid seel with wanton dullness
My speculative and officed instruments,[15]

---

[1] **To . . . ear:** listen to my story with a favorable ear. [2] **charter:** pledge. [3] **downright violence:** unbridled impetuosity. [4] **subdued:** conquered. [5] **quality:** calling (soldier). [6] **I saw . . . mind:** that is, his good qualities overshadowed his looks. [7] **his valiant parts:** his prowess in battle. [8] **heavy:** sad. [9] **voices:** approval. [10] **heat:** lust. [11] **young effects:** youthful passions. [12] **mind:** wishes. [13] **scant:** neglect. [14] **For:** because. [15] **seel . . . instruments:** close my eyes to duty.

That my disports corrupt and taint my business,
Let housewives make a skillet of my helm,[1]
And all indign[2] and base adversities
Make head [3] against my estimation! [4]

DUKE.

Be it as you shall privately determine,
Either for her stay or going: th'affair cries haste.
And speed must answer it.

FIRST SENATOR.

You must away to-night.

OTHELLO.

With all my heart.

DUKE.

At nine i'the morning here we'll meet again.—
Othello, leave some officer behind,
And he shall our commission bring to you;
With such things else of quality and respect
As doth import you.[5]

OTHELLO.

So please your Grace, my ancient;
A man he is of honesty and trust:
To his conveyance[6] I assign my wife,
With what else needful your good Grace shall think
To be sent after me.

DUKE.

Let it be so.—
Good night to every one.—[*to* BRABANTIO] And, noble signior,
If virtue no delighted [7] beauty lack,
Your son-in-law is far more fair than black.

FIRST SENATOR.

Adieu, brave Moor: use Desdemona well.

---

[1] **helm:** helmet. [2] **indign:** disgraceful. [3] **Make head:** join in the attack. [4] **estimation:** reputation. [5] **doth import you:** are of concern or importance to you. [6] **conveyance:** escort. [7] **delighted:** delightful.

BRABANTIO.

Look to her, Moor, if thou hast eyes to see:
She has deceived her father, and may thee.

[*Exeunt* DUKE, SENATORS, OFFICERS, *&c.*

OTHELLO.

My life upon her faith!—Honest Iago,
My Desdemona must I leave to thee:
I prithee,[1] let thy wife attend on her;
And bring them after in the best advantage.[2]—
Come, Desdemona; I have but an hour
Of love, of worldly matters and direction,
To spend with thee: we must obey the time.

[*Exeunt* OTHELLO *and* DESDEMONA.

RODERIGO.

Iago,—

IAGO.

What say'st thou, noble heart?

RODERIGO.

What will I do, think'st thou?

IAGO.

Why, go to bed, and sleep.

RODERIGO.

I will incontinently[3] drown myself.

IAGO.

If thou dost, I shall never love thee after. Why, thou silly gentleman!

RODERIGO.

It is silliness to live when to live is torment; and then have we a prescription to die when death is our physician.

IAGO.

O villainous! I have lookt upon the world for four times seven years; and since I could distinguish betwixt a benefit and an

---

[1] prithee: pray thee.
[2] in the best advantage: at the best opportunity.
[3] incontinently: immediately.

injury, I never found man that knew how to love himself. Ere I would say, I would drown myself for the love of a guinea-hen,[1] I would change my humanity with a baboon.

RODERIGO.

What should I do? I confess it is my shame to be so fond; but it is not in my virtue[2] to amend it.

IAGO.

Virtue! a fig! 'tis in ourselves that we are thus or thus. Our bodies are gardens; to the which our wills are gardeners: so that if we will plant nettles, or sow lettuce; set hyssop,[3] and weed-up thyme; supply it with one gender of herbs, or distract[4] it with many; either to have it sterile with idleness, or manured with industry; why, the power and corrigible[5] authority of this lies in our wills. If the balance of our lives had not one scale of reason to poise another of sensuality, the blood and baseness of our natures would conduct us to most preposterous conclusions: but we have reason to cool our raging motions, our carnal strings, our unbitted[6] lusts; whereof I take this that you call love to be a sect or scion.[7]

RODERIGO.

It cannot be.

IAGO.

It is merely a lust of the blood and a permission of the will. Come, be a man: drown thyself! drown cats and blind puppies. I have profest me thy friend, and I confess me knit to thy deserving with cables of perdurable[8] toughness; I could never better stead[9] thee than now. Put money in thy purse;

---

[1] **guinea-hen:** an old term for prostitute. [2] **virtue:** character. [3] **hyssop:** an old-fashioned herb. [4] **distract:** vary. [5] **corrigible:** that is, capable of being corrected. [6] **unbitted:** unbridled; uncontrolled. [7] **sect or scion:** cutting or offshoot. [8] **perdurable:** lasting; enduring. [9] **stead:** serve.

follow thou the wars; defeat thy favour with an usurpt beard;[1] I say, put money in thy purse. It cannot be that Desdemona should long continue her love to the Moor,—put money in thy purse,—nor he his to her: it was a violent commencement, and thou shalt see an answerable sequestration;[2]—put but money in thy purse.—These Moors are changeable in their wills:[3]—fill thy purse with money:—the food that to him now is as luscious as locusts[4] shall be to him shortly as bitter as coloquintida.[5] She must change for youth; when she is sated with his body, she will find the error of her choice: she must have change, she must: therefore put money in thy purse.—If thou wilt needs damn thyself, do it a more delicate way than drowning. Make all the money thou canst: if sanctimony and a frail vow betwixt an erring[6] barbarian and a supersubtle Venetian be not too hard for my wits and all the tribe of hell, thou shalt enjoy her; therefore make money. A pox of drowning thyself! it is clean out of the way:[7] seek thou rather to be hang'd in compassing[8] thy joy than to be drown'd and go without her.

RODERIGO.

Wilt thou be fast [9] to my hopes, if I depend on the issue?

IAGO.

Thou art sure of me:—go, make money:—I have told thee often, and I re-tell thee again and again, I hate the Moor: my cause is hearted:[10] thine hath no less reason. Let us be conjunctive in our revenge against him: if thou canst cuckold him, thou dost thyself a pleasure, me a sport. There are many

---

[1] **defeat thy favour with an usurpt beard:** disguise your appearance by wearing a false beard. [2] **sequestration:** separation. [3] **wills:** desires. [4] **locusts:** fruit of the locust tree. [5] **coloquintida:** a bitter purgative. [6] **erring:** errant; roving. [7] **clean out of the way:** entirely out of the question. [8] **compassing:** encompassing; achieving. [9] **fast:** loyal. [10] **hearted:** from the heart.

events in the womb of time, which will be deliver'd. Traverse;[1] go; provide thy money. We will have more of this to-morrow. Adieu.

RODERIGO.

Where shall we meet i'the morning?

IAGO.

At my lodging.

RODERIGO.

I'll be with thee betimes.[2]

IAGO.

Go to; farewell. Do you hear, Roderigo?

RODERIGO.

What say you?

IAGO.

No more of drowning, do you hear?

RODERIGO.

I am changed: I'll go sell all my land.

IAGO.

Go to; farewell! put money in your purse.

[*Exit* RODERIGO.

Thus do I ever make my fool my purse;[3]
For I mine own gain'd knowledge should profane,
If I would time expend with such a snipe,[4]
But for my sport and profit. I hate the Moor;
And it is thought abroad,[5] that 'twixt my sheets
'Has done my office.[6] I know not if't be true;
But I, for mere suspicion in that kind,
Will do as if for surety.[7] He holds me well;[8]
The better shall my purpose work on him.
Cassio's a proper man: let me see now;
To get his place, and to plume up my will

---

[1] **Traverse:** turn around and march. [2] **betimes:** early. [3] **make my fool my purse:** use a fool for my own gain. [4] **snipe:** contemptible fellow (an insignificant bird). [5] **thought abroad:** common knowledge. [6] **'twixt . . . office:** Iago suspects his own wife of infidelity with Othello. [7] **Will do as if for surety:** will act as if it is a certainty. [8] **He holds me well:** he thinks well of me.

In double knavery—How, how?—Let's see:—
After some time, to abuse Othello's ear
That he is too familiar with his wife:—
He hath a person,[1] and a smooth dispose,[2]
To be suspected; framed [3] to make women false.
The Moor is of a free and open nature,
That thinks men honest that but seem to be so;
And will as tenderly[4] be led by th' nose
As asses are.
I have't;—it is engender'd:—hell and night
Must bring this monstrous birth to the world's light.

[*Exit.*

---

[1] **a person:** good looks.
[2] **a smooth dispose:** gallant or charming manners, which leave him open to suspicion.
[3] **framed:** designed.
[4] **tenderly:** easily; unresistingly.

Othello

ACT 2

ACT II

DESDEMONA and Iago arrive at Cyprus directly after Othello. Where Cassio elegantly addresses the arrivals, Iago is the bluntly spoken, coarsely joking soldier. Othello, in greeting his wife, declares his whole world to depend on her. But during that evening's celebration of the general's marriage, for providentially a storm has scattered the Turkish fleet, all this is to change. Iago uses his camaraderie and his soldier's jests to pump Cassio full of drink. Cassio is not only found drunk on duty but brawling as well. Roderigo stirs up an easy fight to the point where Cassio wounds a leading Cypriot in the brawl. Othello is furious at discovering his lieutenant in this shameful predicament and dismisses him instantly. Iago, always the friend, has immediate advice for the humiliated Cassio—to seek out Desdemona to intercede with her husband for him.

ACT II. SCENE I.

A seaport town in Cyprus. An open place near the Quay.

Enter MONTANO *and two* GENTLEMEN.

MONTANO.

What from the cape can you discern at sea?

FIRST GENTLEMAN.

Nothing at all: it is a high-wrought flood;[1]
I cannot 'twixt the heaven and the main
Descry a sail.

MONTANO.

Methinks the wind hath spoke aloud at land;
A fuller blast ne'er shook our battlements:
If it hath ruffian'd so upon the sea,
What ribs of oak, when mountains melt on them,
Can hold the mortise? [2] What shall we hear of this?

SECOND GENTLEMAN.

A segregation[3] of the Turkish fleet:
For do but stand upon the foaming shore,
The chiding[4] billow seems to pelt the clouds;

---

[1] **high-wrought flood:** stormy sea.
[2] **hold the mortise:** hold together at the joints.
[3] **segregation:** dispersion or separation.
[4] **chiding:** brawling.

The wind-shaked surge, with high and monstrous mane,
Seems to cast water on the burning bear,[1]
And quench the guards of th'ever-fixed pole:[2]
I never did like molestation view
On the enchafed flood.[3]

MONTANO.

If that the Turkish fleet
Be not enshelter'd and embay'd, they are drown'd;
It is impossible they bear it out.[4]

Enter a third GENTLEMAN.

THIRD GENTLEMAN.

News, lads! our wars are done.
The desperate tempest hath so bang'd the Turks,
That their designment [5] halts: a noble ship of Venice
Hath seen a grievous wrack[6] and sufferance[7]
On most part of their fleet.

MONTANO.

How! is this true?

THIRD GENTLEMAN.

The ship is here put in,
A Veronesa; Michael Cassio,
Lieutenant to the warlike Moor Othello,
Is come on shore: the Moor himself's at sea,
And is in full commission here for Cyprus.

MONTANO.

I am glad on't; 'tis a worthy governor.

THIRD GENTLEMAN.

But this same Cassio, though he speak of comfort
Touching the Turkish loss, yet he looks sadly,
And prays the Moor be safe; for they were parted

---

[1] **burning bear:** the constellation ursa minor. [2] **guards of th'ever-fixed pole:** the two bright stars that seem to stand as guards of the North Star (Polaris). [3] **I never did like molestation view/On the enchafed flood:** I have never seen such a turbulent and angry sea. [4] **bear it out:** that is, ride out the storm. [5] **designment:** battle plans. [6] **wrack:** wreck. [7] **sufferance:** damage.

With foul and violent tempest.

MONTANO.

Pray heaven he be;
For I have served him, and the man commands
Like a full [1] soldier. Let's to the seaside, ho!
As well to see the vessel that's come in
As to throw out our eyes for brave Othello,
Even till we make the main and th'aerial blue
An indistinct regard.[2]

THIRD GENTLEMAN.

Come, let's do so;
For every minute is expectancy
Of more arrivance.[3]

Enter CASSIO.

CASSIO.

Thanks, you the valiant of this warlike isle,
That so approve the Moor! O, let the heavens
Give him defence against the elements,
For I have lost him on a dangerous sea!

MONTANO.

Is he well shipt? [4]

CASSIO.

His bark is stoutly timber'd, and his pilot
Of very expert and approved allowance;[5]
Therefore my hopes, not surfeited to death,
Stand in bold cure.[6]

[*within*] A sail, a sail, a sail!

Enter a fourth GENTLEMAN.

CASSIO.

What noise?

FOURTH GENTLEMAN.

The town is empty; on the brow o'the sea
Stand ranks of people, and they cry 'A sail!'

---

[1] **full:** complete. [2] **we make the main and th'aerial blue/An indistinct regard:** that is, the sea and sky merge. [3] **arrivance:** arrivals. [4] **Is he well shipt:** has he a stout ship. [5] **approved allowance:** "allowed and approved expertness"—Steevens. [6] **my hopes, not surfeited to death,/Stand in bold cure:** that is, my hopes (for his return)—not yet extinguished—may be fully realized.

CASSIO.

My hopes do shape him for the governor. [*Guns within.*

SECOND GENTLEMAN.

They do discharge their shot of courtesy:
Our friends at least.

CASSIO.

I pray you, sir, go forth,
And give us truth who 'tis that is arrived.

SECOND GENTLEMAN.

I shall. [*Exit.*

MONTANO.

But, good lieutenant, is your general wived? [1]

CASSIO.

Most fortunately: he hath achieved a maid
That paragons description and wild fame;[2]
One that excels the quirks of blazoning pens,[3]
And in th' essential vesture of creation
Does tire the ingener.[4]

Enter second GENTLEMAN.

How now! who has put in?

SECOND GENTLEMAN.

'Tis one Iago, ancient to the general.

CASSIO.

'Has had most favourable and happy speed:
Tempests themselves, high seas, and howling winds,
The gutter'd [5] rocks, and congregated [6] sands,—
Traitors ensteept[7] to clog the guiltless keel,—
As having sense of beauty, do omit [8]
Their mortal [9] natures, letting go safely by
The divine Desdemona.

MONTANO.

What is she?

---

[1] **wived:** married. [2] **paragons description and wild fame:** surpasses anyone's ability to describe and extravagant publicity. [3] **quirks of blazoning pens:** ingenious inventions of flattering pens. [4] **in the . . . ingener:** in the form given by the Creator tires the imagination to describe. [5] **gutter'd:** jagged. [6] **congregated:** heaped up. [7] **ensteept:** sunken; hidden. [8] **omit:** forget. [9] **mortal** deadly.

CASSIO.

She that I spake of, our great captain's captain,
Left in the conduct of the bold Iago;
Whose footing[1] here anticipates our thoughts
A se'nnight's[2] speed.—Great Jove, Othello guard,
And swell his sail with thine own powerful breath,
That he may bless this bay with his tall [3] ship,
Make love's quick pants in Desdemona's arms,
Give renew'd fire to our extincted [4] spirits,
And bring all Cyprus comfort!—O, behold,

Enter DESDEMONA, EMILIA, IAGO, RODERIGO, *and* ATTENDANTS.

The riches of the ship is come on shore!
Ye men of Cyprus, let her have your knees.—
Hail to thee, lady! and the grace of heaven
Before, behind thee, and on every hand,
Enwheel [5] thee round!

DESDEMONA.

I thank you, valiant Cassio.
What tidings can you tell me of my lord?

CASSIO.

He is not yet arrived: nor know I aught
But that he's well, and will be shortly here.

DESDEMONA.

O, but I fear—How lost you company?

CASSIO.

The great contention of the sea and skies
Parted our fellowship:—but, hark! a sail.
[*within*] A sail, a sail! [*Guns within.*

SECOND GENTLEMAN.

They give their greeting to the citadel:
This likewise is a friend.

---

[1] footing: landing.
[2] se'nnight: seven nights (a week).
[3] tall: stout; fine.
[4] extincted: extinguished.
[5] Enwheel: encircle.

CASSIO.

See for the news.—

[*Exit* GENTLEMAN.

Good ancient, you are welcome:—[*to* EMILIA] welcome, mistress:—
Let it not gall your patience, good Iago,
That I extend my manners; 'tis my breeding
That gives me this bold show of courtesy. [*Kissing her.*

IAGO.

Sir, would she give you so much of her lips
As of her tongue she oft bestows on me,
You'ld have enough.

DESDEMONA.

Alas, she has no speech.

IAGO.

In faith, too much;
I find it still,[1] when I have list [2] to sleep:
Marry, before your ladyship, I grant,
She puts her tongue a little in her heart,
And chides with thinking.[3]

EMILIA.

You have little cause to say so.

IAGO.

Come on, come on; you are pictures[4] out of doors,
Bells in your parlours,[5] wild-cats in your kitchens,
Saints in your injuries,[6] devils being offended,
Players[7] in your housewifery, and housewives[8] in your beds.

DESDEMONA.

O, fie upon thee, slanderer!

IAGO.

Nay, it is true, or else I am a Turk:

---

[1] **still:** so. [2] **have list:** desire; wish. [3] **chides with thinking:** scolds without reason. [4] **pictures:** models of propriety. [5] **Bells in your parlours:** talk with voices as pleasing as tinkling bells when entertaining. [6] **Saints in your injuries:** that is, you put on an air of sanctity when you have hurt others. [7] **Players:** idlers. [8] **housewives:** hussies.

You rise to play, and go to bed to work.

EMILIA.

You shall not write my praise.

IAGO.

No, let me not.

DESDEMONA.

What wouldst thou write of me, if thou shouldst praise me?

IAGO.

O gentle lady, do not put me to't;
For I am nothing, if not critical.

DESDEMONA.

Come on, assay.[1]—There's one gone to the harbour?

IAGO.

Ay, madam.

DESDEMONA.

I am not merry; but I do beguile
The thing I am, by seeming otherwise.—
Come, how wouldst thou praise me?

IAGO.

I am about it; but, indeed, my invention[2]
Comes from my pate as birdlime[3] does from frize,[4]—
It plucks out brains and all: but my Muse labours,
And thus she is deliver'd.
If she be fair and wise,—fairness and wit,
The one's for use, the other useth it.[5]

DESDEMONA.

Well praised! How if she be black[6] and witty?

IAGO.

If she be black, and thereto have a wit,
She'll find a white that shall her blackness fit.[7]

---

[1] **assay:** make an attempt. [2] **invention:** thoughts. [3] **birdlime:** a sticky substance used to snare birds. [4] **frize:** frieze—a coarse cloth with a shaggy nap on one side. [5] **The one's for use, the other useth it:** that is, her wit makes full use of her beauty. [6] **black:** ugly. [7] **If she be black . . . fit:** even though she is ugly, if she is clever, she will find someone to love her.

DESDEMONA.

Worse and worse.

EMILIA.

How if fair and foolish?

IAGO.

She never yet was foolish that was fair;
For even her folly helpt her to an heir.

DESDEMONA.

These are old fond [1] paradoxes to make fools laugh i'th'alehouse. What miserable praise hast thou for her that's foul and foolish?

IAGO.

There's none so foul, and foolish thereunto,
But does foul pranks which fair and wise ones do.

DESDEMONA.

O heavy ignorance!—thou praisest the worst best. But what praise couldst thou bestow on a deserving woman indeed,—one that, in the authority of her merit, did justly put on the vouch of very malice itself? [2]

IAGO.

She that was ever fair, and never proud;
Had tongue at will,[3] and yet was never loud;
Never lackt gold, and yet went never gay;[4]
Fled from her wish, and yet said 'Now I may;'
She that, being anger'd, her revenge being nigh,
Bade her wrong stay, and her displeasure fly;
She that in wisdom never was so frail
To change the cod's head for the salmon's tail;[5]
She that could think, and ne'er disclose her mind;
See suitors following, and not look behind;
She was a wight,[6] if ever such wight were,—

---

[1] **fond:** foolish. [2] **one . . . itself:** a woman so conscious of her own virtue that even the most malicious were forced to put their stamp of approval on her. [3] **Had tongue at will:** could easily express her thoughts. [4] **gay:** showy; ostentatious. [5] **To change the cod's head for the salmon's tail:** to exchange a delicacy for coarser fare (Othello). [6] **wight:** person.

DESDEMONA.

To do what?

IAGO.

To suckle fools and chronicle small beer.[1]

DESDEMONA.

O most lame and impotent conclusion!—Do not learn of him, Emilia, though he be thy husband.—How say you, Cassio? is he not a most profane[2] and liberal [3] counsellor?

CASSIO.

He speaks home,[4] madam: you may relish him more in the soldier than in the scholar.

IAGO [*aside*].

He takes her by the palm: ay, well said, whisper: with as little a web as this will I ensnare as great a fly as Cassio. Ay, smile upon her, do; I will gyve thee in thine own courtship. You say true; 'tis so, indeed; if such tricks as these strip you out of your lieutenantry, it had been better you had not kist your three fingers so oft, which now again you are most apt to play the sir in. Very good; well kist! an excellent courtesy! 'tis so, indeed. Yet again your fingers to your lips? would they were clyster-pipes[5] for your sake! [*Trumpet within*]—The Moor! I know his trumpet.

CASSIO.

'Tis truly so.

DESDEMONA.

Let's meet him, and receive him.

CASSIO.

Lo, where he comes!

Enter OTHELLO *and* ATTENDANTS.

OTHELLO.

O my fair warrior! [6]

---

[1] **chronicle small beer:** keep household accounts (a menial occupation). [2] **profane:** coarse of language. [3] **liberal:** licentious. [4] **He speaks home:** his words strike home (with the truth). [5] **clyster-pipes:** enema tubes. [6] **warrior:** an allusion to Desdemona's following him to the wars.

DESDEMONA.

My dear Othello!

OTHELLO.

It gives me wonder great as my content
To see you here before me. O my soul's joy!
If after every tempest come such calms,
May the winds blow till they have waken'd death!
And let the labouring bark climb hills of seas
Olympus-high, and duck again as low
As hell's from heaven! If it were now to die,
'Twere now to be most happy; for, I fear,
My soul hath her content so absolute,
That not another comfort [1] like to this
Succeeds[2] in unknown fate.

DESDEMONA.

The heavens forbid
But that our loves and comforts should increase,
Even as our days do grow!

OTHELLO.

Amen to that, sweet powers!
I cannot speak enough of this content;
It stops me here; it is too much of joy:
And this, and this, the greatest discords be

[*Kissing her*.

That e'er our hearts shall make!

IAGO [*aside*].

O, you are well tuned now!
But I'll set down the pegs[3] that make this music,
As honest as I am.

OTHELLO.

Come, let us to the castle.—
News, friends; our wars are done, the Turks are drown'd.

---

[1] **comfort:** happiness; delight.
[2] **succeeds:** follows.
[3] **set down the pegs:** loosen the strings (and thus put out of tune).

How does my old acquaintance of this isle?—
Honey, you shall be well desired [1] in Cyprus;
I have found great love amongst them. O my sweet,
I prattle out of fashion,[2] and I dote[3]
In mine own comforts.—I prithee, good Iago,
Go to the bay and disembark my coffers:
Bring thou the master to the citadel;
He is a good one, and his worthiness
Does challenge much respect.—Come, Desdemona,
Once more well met at Cyprus.

[*Exeunt* OTHELLO, DESDEMONA, *and* ATTENDANTS.

IAGO.

Do thou meet me presently at the harbour. Come hither. If thou be'st valiant,—as, they say, base men being in love have then a nobility in their natures more than is native to them,—list me.[4] The lieutenant to-night watches on the court-of-guard:[5]—first, I must tell thee this—Desdemona is directly[6] in love with him.

RODERIGO.

With him! why, 'tis not possible.

IAGO.

Lay thy finger thus,[7] and let thy soul be instructed. Mark me with what violence[8] she first loved the Moor, but for bragging, and telling her fantastical lies: and will she love him still for prating? let not thy discreet heart think it. Her eye must be fed; and what delight shall she have to look on the devil? When the blood is made dull with the act of sport, there should be—again to inflame it, and to give

---

[1] **desired:** catered to; loved. [2] **out of fashion:** unsuitably; irrationally. [3] **dote:** revel foolishly. [4] **list me:** listen to me. [5] **court-of-guard:** guardhouse; mustering place of the guard. [6] **directly:** truly. [7] **Lay thy finger thus:** put your finger across your mouth (for silence). [8] **violence:** ardor.

satiety a fresh appetite—loveliness in favour,[1] sympathy in years,[2] manners, and beauties; all which the Moor is defective in: now, for want of these required conveniences, her delicate tenderness will find itself abused, begin to heave the gorge,[3] disrelish and abhor the Moor; very[4] nature will instruct her in it, and compel her to some second choice. Now, sir, this granted,—as it is a most pregnant[5] and unforced position,—who stands so eminent in the degree of this fortune as Cassio does? a knave very voluble; no further conscionable[6] than in putting on the mere form of civil and humane seeming, for the better compassing of his salt [7] and most hidden loose affection? why, none; why, none: a slipper[8] and subtle knave; a finder of occasions; that has an eye can stamp and counterfeit advantages, though true advantage never present itself: a devilish knave! Besides, the knave is handsome, young, and hath all those requisites in him that folly and green minds[9] look after: a pestilent complete knave; and the woman hath found him already.

RODERIGO.

I cannot believe that in her; she's full of most blest condition.

IAGO.

Blest fig's-end! the wine she drinks is made of grapes:[10] if she had been blest, she would never have loved the Moor: blest pudding! Didst thou not see her paddle[11] with the palm of his hand? didst not mark that?

RODERIGO.

Yes, that I did; but that was but courtesy.

---

[1] **favour:** face; appearance. [2] **sympathy in years:** that is, near the same age. [3] **heave the gorge:** vomit. [4] **very:** mere. [5] **pregnant:** full of conviction. [6] **no further conscionable:** with no more conscience. [7] **salt:** lecherous. [8] **slipper:** slippery. [9] **green minds:** minds not fully developed. [10] **the wine . . . grapes:** that is, she is as prone to human failings as anyone. [11] **paddle:** pat gently.

IAGO.

Lechery, by this hand; an index[1] and obscure prologue to the history of lust and foul thoughts. They met so near with their lips, that their breaths embraced together. Villainous thoughts, Roderigo! when these mutualities[2] so marshal [3] the way, hard at hand comes the master and main exercise, the incorporate conclusion: pish!—But, sir, be you ruled [4] by me: I have brought you from Venice. Watch you to-night; for the command, I'll lay't upon you: Cassio knows you not:—I'll not be far from you: do you find some occasion to anger Cassio, either by speaking too loud, or tainting[5] his discipline; or from what other course you please, which the time shall more favourably minister.[6]

RODERIGO.

Well.

IAGO.

Sir, he is rash, and very sudden in choler,[7] and haply may strike at you: provoke him, that he may; for even out of that will I cause these of Cyprus to mutiny; whose qualification shall come into no true taste again[8] but by the displanting of Cassio. So shall you have a shorter journey to your desires, by the means I shall then have to prefer[9] them; and the impediment most profitably removed, without the which there were no expectation of our prosperity.

RODERIGO.

I will do this, if I can bring it to any opportunity.

IAGO.

I warrant thee. Meet me by and by at the citadel: I must fetch his necessaries ashore. Farewell.

---

[1] **index:** the index was placed at the beginning of the text in Shakespeare's day. [2] **mutualities:** exchanges of loving or polite expressions. [3] **marshal:** usher; lead. [4] **ruled:** guided. [5] **tainting:** throwing a slur upon. [6] **minister:** supply. [7] **choler:** anger. [8] **whose qualification . . . again:** whose pacification or appeasement will retain some bitterness. [9] **prefer:** advance; promote.

RODERIGO.

Adieu. [*Exit.*

IAGO.

That Cassio loves her, I do well believe it;
That she loves him, 'tis apt, and of great credit:[1]
The Moor—howbeit that [2] I endure him not—
Is of a constant, loving, noble nature;
And I dare think he'll prove to Desdemona
A most dear husband. Now, I do love her too;
Not out of absolute lust,—though peradventure
I stand accountant for as great a sin,—
But partly led to diet [3] my revenge,
For that I do suspect the lusty Moor
Hath leapt into my seat: the thought whereof
Doth, like a poisonous mineral, gnaw my inwards;
And nothing can or shall content my soul
Till I am even'd with him, wife for wife;
Or failing so, yet that I put the Moor
At least into a jealousy so strong
That judgement cannot cure. Which thing to do,
If this poor trash[4] of Venice, whom I trash
For his quick hunting, stand the putting on,
I'll have our Michael Cassio on the hip;[5]
Abuse him to the Moor in the rank garb,[6]—
For I fear Cassio with my night-cap too;
Make the Moor thank me, love me, and reward me,
For making him egregiously[7] an ass,
And practising upon[8] his peace and quiet
Even to madness. 'Tis here, but yet confused:
Knavery's plain face is never seen till used. [*Exit.*

---

[1] **of great credit:** entirely believable. [2] **howbeit that:** although. [3] **diet:** feed. [4] **trash:** in hunting, to restrain a dog by a leash. [5] **on the hip:** a term in wrestling, meaning at a disadvantage. [6] **the rank garb:** a direct or brutal manner (with a play on the word *rank* as lascivious). [7] **egregiously:** eminently. [8] **practising upon:** scheming against.

SCENE II.

A street.

Enter OTHELLO'S HERALD *with a proclamation;* PEOPLE *following.*

HERALD.
It is Othello's pleasure, our noble and valiant general, that, upon certain tidings now arrived, importing the mere perdition[1] of the Turkish fleet, every man put himself into triumph; some to dance, some to make bonfires, each man to what sport and revels his addiction leads him: for, besides these beneficial news, it is the celebration of his nuptial:—so much was his pleasure should be proclaim'd. All offices[2] are open; and there is full liberty of feasting from this present hour of five till the bell have told eleven. Heaven bless the isle of Cyprus and our noble general Othello! [*Exeunt.*

SCENE III.

A hall in the castle.

Enter OTHELLO, DESDEMONA, CASSIO, *and* ATTENDANTS.

OTHELLO.
Good Michael, look you to the guard to-night:
Let's teach ourselves that honourable stop,[3]
Not to outsport discretion.

CASSIO.
Iago hath direction what to do;
But, notwithstanding, with my personal eye
Will I look to't.

---

[1] **mere perdition:** complete destruction.
[2] **offices:** kitchens; storerooms; Halliwell says "the rooms appropriated to the upper servants of great families."
[3] **stop:** restraint.

OTHELLO.

Iago is most honest.
Michael, good night: to-morrow with your earliest
Let me have speech with you.—[*to* DESDEMONA]
Come, my dear love,—
The purchase made, the fruits are to ensue;
That profit's yet to come 'twixt me and you.—
Good night.

[*Exeunt* OTHELLO, DESDEMONA, *and* ATTENDANTS.

Enter IAGO.

CASSIO.

Welcome, Iago; we must to the watch.

IAGO.

Not this hour, lieutenant; 'tis not yet ten o'the clock. Our general cast [1] us thus early for the love of his Desdemona; who let us not therefore blame; he hath not yet made wanton the night with her; and she is sport for Jove.

CASSIO.

She's a most exquisite lady.

IAGO.

And, I'll warrant her, full of game.[2]

CASSIO.

Indeed, she's a most fresh and delicate creature.

IAGO.

What an eye she has! methinks it sounds a parley to provocation.

CASSIO.

An inviting eye; and yet methinks right modest.

IAGO.

And when she speaks, is it not an alarum[3] to love?

---

[1] cast: dismissed.
[2] game: amorous play.
[3] alarum: call.

CASSIO.

She is, indeed, perfection.

IAGO.

Well, happiness to their sheets! Come, lieutenant, I have a stoop[1] of wine; and here without are a brace of Cyprus gallants that would fain have a measure[2] to the health of black Othello.

CASSIO.

Not to-night, good Iago: I have very poor and unhappy brains for drinking: I could well wish courtesy would invent some other custom of entertainment.

IAGO.

O, they are our friends; but one cup: I'll drink for you.

CASSIO.

I have drunk but one cup to-night, and that was craftily qualified [3] too, and, behold, what innovation[4] it makes here: I am unfortunate in the infirmity, and dare not task my weakness with any more.

IAGO.

What, man! 'tis a night of revels: the gallants desire it.

CASSIO.

Where are they?

IAGO.

Here at the door; I pray you, call them in.

CASSIO.

I'll do't; but it dislikes me.[5] [*Exit.*

IAGO.

If I can fasten but one cup upon him,
With that which he hath drunk to-night already,
He'll be as full of quarrel and offence

---

[1] **stoop:** a large tankard.
[2] **measure:** draught.
[3] **craftily qualified:** slyly mixed with water (diluted).
[4] **innovation:** a change.
[5] **it dislikes me:** I dislike it.

As my young mistress' dog. Now, my sick fool Roderigo,
Whom love hath turn'd almost the wrong side out,
To Desdemona hath to-night caroused
Potations pottle[1]-deep; and he's to watch:
Three lads of Cyprus—noble swelling spirits,
That hold their honours in a wary distance,[2]
The very elements of this warlike isle—
Have I to-night fluster'd [3] with flowing cups,
And they watch too. Now, 'mongst this flock of drunkards
Am I to put our Cassio in some action
That may offend the isle:—but here they come:
If consequence[4] do but approve my dream,[5]
My boat sails freely, both with wind and stream.

Enter CASSIO, MONTANO, *and* GENTLEMEN;
SERVANTS *following with wine.*

CASSIO.
'Fore God, they have given me a rouse[6] already.

MONTANO.
Good faith, a little one; not past a pint, as I am a soldier.

IAGO.
Some wine, ho! [*Sings.*
And let me the canakin clink, clink;
And let me the canakin clink;
A soldier's a man;
A life's but a span;
Why, then, let a soldier drink.
Some wine, boys!

CASSIO.
'Fore God, an excellent song.

---

[1] **pottle:** a tankard holding two quarts. [2] **hold their honours in a wary distance:** that is, are quick to take offense if their honor is questioned. [3] **fluster'd:** befuddled by drinking. [4] **consequence:** subsequent events. [5] **dream:** scheme. [6] **a rouse:** full glass downed.

IAGO.

I learn'd it in England, where, indeed, they are most potent in potting:[1] your Dane, your German, and your swag-bellied[2] Hollander,—Drink, ho!—are nothing to your English.

CASSIO.

Is your Englishman so expert in his drinking?

IAGO.

Why, he drinks you, with facility, your Dane dead drunk; he sweats not to overthrow your Almain;[3] he gives your Hollander a vomit, ere the next pottle can be fill'd.

CASSIO.

To the health of our general!

MONTANO.

I am for it, lieutenant; and I'll do you justice.

IAGO.

O sweet England! [*Sings*

King Stephen was a worthy peer,
His breeches cost him but a crown;
He held them sixpence all too dear,
With that he call'd the tailor lown.[4]

He was a wight[5] of high renown,
And thou art but of low degree:
'Tis pride that pulls the country down;
Then take thine auld cloak about thee.

Some wine, ho!

CASSIO.

Why, this is a more exquisite song than the other.

IAGO.

Will you hear't again?

CASSIO.

No; for I hold him to be unworthy of his place that does those things.—Well,—God's above all; and there be souls must be saved, and there be souls must not be saved.

---

[1] **potting:** heavy drinking.
[2] **swag-bellied:** pot-bellied.
[3] **sweats not to overthrow your Almain:** has no difficulty in out-drinking a German.
[4] **lown:** lout.
[5] **wight:** person.

IAGO.

It's true, good lieutenant.

CASSIO.

For mine own part,—no offence to the general, nor any man of quality,—I hope to be saved.

IAGO.

And so do I too, lieutenant.

CASSIO.

Ay, but, by your leave, not before me; the lieutenant is to be saved before the ancient. Let's have no more of this; let's to our affairs.—God forgive us our sins!—Gentlemen, let's look to our business. Do not think, gentlemen, I am drunk: this is my ancient;—This is my right hand, and this is my left:—I am not drunk now; I can stand well enough, and speak well enough.

ALL.

Excellent well.

CASSIO.

Why, very well, then; you must not think, then, that I am drunk. [*Exit.*

MONTANO.

To the platform,[1] masters; come, let's set the watch.

IAGO.

You see this fellow that is gone before;—
He is a soldier fit to stand by Cæsar
And give direction: and do but see his vice;
'Tis to his virtue a just equinox,[2]
The one as long as th'other: 'tis pity of him.
I fear the trust Othello puts him in,

---

[1] **platform:** where the guards watched.
[2] **equinox:** equal; counterpart.

On some odd time of his infirmity,
Will shake this island.

MONTANO.

But is he often thus?

IAGO.

'Tis evermore the prologue to his sleep:
He'll watch the horologe[1] a double set,[2]
If drink rock not his cradle.

MONTANO.

It were well
The general were put in mind of it.
Perhaps he sees it not; or his good nature
Prizes the virtue that appears in Cassio,
And looks not on his evils: is not this true?

Enter RODERIGO.

IAGO [*aside to* RODERIGO].
How now, Roderigo!
I pray you, after the lieutenant; go. [*Exit* RODERIGO.

MONTANO.
And 'tis great pity that the noble Moor
Should hazard such a place as his own second
With one of an ingraft[3] infirmity:
It were an honest action to say
So to the Moor.

IAGO.

Not I, for this fair island:
I do love Cassio well; and would do much
To cure him of this evil—But, hark! what noise?
[*Cry within,*—'Help! Help!'

Enter CASSIO, *driving in* RODERIGO.

CASSIO.
Zounds, you rogue! you rascal!

---

[1] **horologe:** an ancient clock.
[2] **a double set:** twenty-four hours; twice around the clock.
[3] **ingraft:** deeply seated; ingrained.

MONTANO.

What's the matter, lieutenant?

CASSIO.

A knave teach me my duty! but I'll beat the knave into a twiggen bottle.[1]

RODERIGO.

Beat me!

CASSIO.

Dost thou prate, rogue? [*Striking* RODERIGO.

MONTANO.

Nay, good lieutenant; I pray you, sir, hold your hand.

CASSIO.

Let me go, sir, or I'll knock you o'er the mazard.[2]

MONTANO.

Come, come, you're drunk.

CASSIO.

Drunk! [*They fight.*

IAGO [*aside to* RODERIGO].

Away, I say, go out; and cry a mutiny! [*Exit* RODERIGO.
Nay, good lieutenant,—God's will, gentlemen;—
Help, ho!—Lieutenant,—sir,—Montano,—sir;—
Help, masters!—Here's a goodly watch indeed!
[*Bell rings.*
Who's that which rings the bell?—Diablo, ho!
The town will rise: God's will, lieutenant, hold;
You will be shamed for ever.

Enter OTHELLO *and* ATTENDANTS.

OTHELLO.

What is the matter here?

MONTANO.

Zounds, I bleed still; I am hurt to the death. [*Faints.*

---

[1] **twiggen bottle:** a bottle with a wicker covering.
[2] **mazard:** head.

OTHELLO.

Hold, for your lives!

IAGO.

Hold, ho! Lieutenant,—sir,—Montano,—gentlemen,—
Have you forgot all sense of place and duty?
Hold! the general speaks to you; hold, hold, for shame!

OTHELLO.

Why, how now, ho! from whence ariseth this?
Are we turn'd Turks, and to ourselves do that
Which heaven hath forbid the Ottomites?
For Christian shame, put by this barbarous brawl:
He that stirs next to carve for his own rage,[1]
Holds his soul light; he dies upon his motion.—
Silence that dreadful bell! it frights the isle
From her propriety.—What is the matter, masters?—
Honest Iago, that look'st dead with grieving,
Speak, who began this? on thy love, I charge thee.

IAGO.

I do not know:—friends all but now, even now,
In quarter,[2] and in terms like bride and groom
Devesting them for bed; and then, but now—
As if some planet had unwitted men[3]—
Swords out, and tilting one at other's breast,
In opposition bloody. I cannot speak
Any beginning to this peevish odds;[4]
And would in action glorious I had lost
Those legs that brought me to a part of it!

OTHELLO.

How comes it, Michael, you are thus forgot? [5]

---

[1] **to carve for his own rage:** to kill out of self-indulgence. [2] **in quarter:** on duty. [3] **some planet had unwitted men:** the influence of some planet had caused men to go mad. [4] **I cannot speak/Any beginning to this peevish odds:** I cannot account for this silly quarrel. [5] **you are thus forgot:** you have so far forgotten yourself.

CASSIO.

I pray you, pardon me; I cannot speak.

OTHELLO.

Worthy Montano, you were wont be civil;
The gravity and stillness[1] of your youth
The world hath noted, and your name is great
In mouths of wisest censure:[2] what's the matter,
That you unlace[3] your reputation thus,
And spend your rich opinion[4] for the name
Of a night-brawler? give me answer to it.

MONTANO.

Worthy Othello, I am hurt to danger:[5]
Your officer, Iago, can inform you—
While I spare speech, which something now offends[6] me—
Of all that I do know: nor know I aught
By me that's said or done amiss this night;
Unless self-charity[7] be sometimes a vice,
And to defend ourselves it be a sin
When violence assails us.

OTHELLO.

Now, by heaven,
My blood begins my safer guides to rule;[8]
And passion, having my best judgement collied,[9]
Assays to lead the way:—if I once stir,
Or do but lift this arm, the best of you
Shall sink in my rebuke.[10] Give me to know
How this foul rout began, who set it on;
And he that is approved in this offence,[11]
Though he had twinn'd with me, both at a birth,
Shall lose me.—What! in a town of war,[12]
Yet wild, the people's hearts brimful of fear,
To manage private and domestic quarrel,

---

[1] **stillness:** seriousness. [2] **censure:** judgment. [3] **unlace:** undo. [4] **spend your rich opinion:** squander your good reputation. [5] **hurt to danger:** critically wounded. [6] **offends:** harms. [7] **self-charity:** love for one's safety. [8] **My blood . . . rule:** my anger begins to overrule caution. [9] **collied:** darkened, as coal. [10] **sink in my rebuke:** fall by my sword. [11] **approved in this offence:** proved guilty of starting this quarrel. [12] **town of war:** garrisoned town.

In night, and on the court and guard of safety! [1]
'Tis monstrous.—Iago, who began't?

MONTANO.

If partially affined, or leagued in office,[2]
Thou dost deliver more or less than truth,
Thou art no soldier.

IAGO.

Touch me not so near:
I had rather have this tongue cut from my mouth
Than it should do offence to Michael Cassio;
Yet, I persuade myself, to speak the truth
Shall nothing wrong him.—Thus it is, general.
Montano and myself being in speech,
There comes a fellow crying out for help;
And Cassio following him with determined sword
To execute upon him.[3] Sir, this gentleman
Steps in to Cassio, and entreats his pause:
Myself the crying fellow did pursue,
Lest by his clamour—as it so fell out—
The town might fall in fright: he, swift of foot,
Outran my purpose; and I return'd the rather
For that I heard the clink and fall of swords,
And Cassio high in oath;[4] which till to-night
I ne'er might say before. When I came back,—
For this was brief,—I found them close together,
At blow and thrust; even as again they were
When you yourself did part them.
More of this matter cannot I report:—
But men are men; the best sometimes forget:—
Though Cassio did some little wrong to him,—
As men in rage strike those that wish them best,—
Yet, surely, Cassio, I believe, received

---

[1] **on the court and guard of safety:** while on duty at the guard-house or platform. [2] **partially affined, or leagued in office:** partial because of being related, or brother-officers. [3] **To execute upon him:** to use against him, either to kill or to demand satisfaction. [4] **high in oath:** cursing loudly.

From him that fled some strange indignity,
Which patience could not pass.

OTHELLO.

I know, Iago,
Thy honesty and love doth mince[1] this matter,
Making it light to Cassio.—Cassio, I love thee;
But never more be officer of mine.—

Enter DESDEMONA, *attended.*

Look, if my gentle love be not raised up! [2]—
I'll make thee an example.

DESDEMONA.

What's the matter?

OTHELLO.

All's well now, sweeting;[3] come away to bed.—
Sir, for your hurts, myself will be your surgeon:
Lead him off. [*Exeunt some with* MONTANO.
Iago, look with care about the town,
And silence[4] those whom this vile brawl distracted.—
Come, Desdemona: 'tis the soldiers' life
To have their balmy slumbers waked with strife.
[*Exeunt all but* IAGO *and* CASSIO.

IAGO.

What, are you hurt, lieutenant?

CASSIO.

Ay, past all surgery.

IAGO.

Marry, heaven forbid!

CASSIO.

Reputation, reputation, reputation! O, I have lost my reputation! I have lost the immortal part of myself, and what remains is bestial.—My reputation, Iago, my reputation!

---

[1] **mince:** make little of.
[2] **raised up:** awakened; aroused.
[3] **sweeting:** a term of endearment, originating from the name of a very sweet apple.
[4] **silence:** quiet.

IAGO.

As I am an honest man, I thought you had received some bodily wound; there is more sense in that than in reputation. Reputation is an idle and most false imposition; oft got without merit, and lost without deserving: you have lost no reputation at all, unless you repute yourself such a loser. What, man! there are ways to recover the general again: you are but now cast in his mood,[1] a punishment more in policy[2] than in malice, even so as one would beat his offenceless dog to affright an imperious lion:[3] sue to him[4] again, and he's yours.

CASSIO.

I will rather sue to be despised than to deceive so good a commander with so slight, so drunken, and so indiscreet an officer. Drunk? and speak parrot? [5] and squabble? swagger? swear? and discourse fustian[6] with one's own shadow?—O thou invisible spirit of wine, if thou hast no name to be known by, let us call thee devil!

IAGO.

What was he that you follow'd with your sword?
What had he done to you?

CASSIO.

I know not.

IAGO.

Is't possible?

CASSIO.

I remember a mass of things, but nothing distinctly; a quarrel, but nothing wherefore.—O God, that men should put an enemy in their mouths to steal away their brains! that we

---

[1] cast in his mood: cast out (dismissed) because of Othello's anger.
[2] in policy: for the sake of military discipline.
[3] imperious lion: in this case, the Army.
[4] sue to him: make up to him, or petition him.
[5] speak parrot: speak words without understanding them.
[6] fustian: nonsense (a coarse cloth of little value).

should, with joy, pleasance,[1] revel, and applause, transform ourselves into beasts!

IAGO.

Why, but you are now well enough: how came you thus recover'd?

CASSIO.

It hath pleased the devil drunkenness to give place to the devil wrath: one unperfectness shows me another, to make me frankly despise myself.

IAGO.

Come, you are too severe a moraler:[2] as the time, the place, and the condition of this country stands, I could heartily wish this had not befaln; but, since it is as it is, mend it for your own good.

CASSIO.

I will ask him for my place again,—he shall tell me I am a drunkard! Had I as many mouths as Hydra,[3] such an answer would stop them all. To be now a sensible man, by and by a fool, and presently[4] a beast! O strange!—Every inordinate cup is unblest, and the ingredient is a devil.

IAGO.

Come, come, good wine is a good familiar[5] creature, if it be well used: exclaim no more against it. And, good lieutenant, I think you think I love you.

CASSIO.

I have well approved [6] it, sir.—I drunk!

IAGO.

You or any man living may be drunk at a time, man. I'll tell you what you shall do. Our general's wife is now the general; —I may say so in this respect, for that he hath devoted and

---

[1] **pleasance:** gaiety. [2] **moraler:** moralist. [3] **Hydra:** a nine-headed monster of Greek mythology, capable of growing two more heads each time one head was cut off without being cauterized. [4] **presently:** soon after. [5] **familiar:** friendly. [6] **approved:** proved.

given up himself to the contemplation, mark, and denotement of her parts and graces:[1]—confess yourself freely to her; importune her help to put you in your place again: she is of so free,[2] so kind, so apt, so blessed a disposition, she holds it a vice in her goodness not to do more than she is requested: this broken joint between you and her husband entreat her to splinter,[3] and, my fortunes against any lay[4] worth naming, this crack of your love shall grow stronger than it was before.

CASSIO.

You advise me well.

IAGO.

I protest, in the sincerity of love and honest kindness.

CASSIO.

I think it freely; and betimes[5] in the morning I will beseech the virtuous Desdemona to undertake for me: I am desperate of my fortunes if they check me here.

IAGO.

You are in the right. Good night, lieutenant; I must to the watch.

CASSIO.

Good night, honest Iago. [*Exit.*

IAGO.

And what's he, then, that says I play the villain?
When this advice is free I give and honest,
Probal to thinking,[6] and, indeed, the course
To win the Moor again? For 'tis most easy
Th'inclining[7] Desdemona to subdue
In any honest suit: she's framed as fruitful
As the free elements. And then for her

---

[1] **denotement of her parts and graces:** devotion to her good qualities and beauty. [2] **free:** generous. [3] **splinter:** splint. [4] **lay:** wager. [5] **betimes:** early. [6] **Probal to thinking:** probable; logical. [7] **inclining:** compliant; inclined to be sympathetic or helpful.

To win the Moor,—were't to renounce his baptism,
All seals and symbols of redeemed sin,
His soul is so enfetter'd to her love,
That she may make, unmake, do what she list,[1]
Even as her appetite[2] shall play the god
With his weak function.[3] How am I, then, a villain
To counsel Cassio to this parallel course,
Directly to his good? Divinity of hell!
When devils will the blackest sins put on,[4]
They do suggest[5] at first with heavenly shows,
As I do now: for whiles this honest fool
Plies[6] Desdemona to repair his fortunes,
And she for him pleads strongly to the Moor,
I'll pour this pestilence into his ear,—
That she repeals him[7] for her body's lust;
And by how much she strives to do him good,
She shall undo her credit with the Moor.
So will I turn her virtue into pitch;[8]
And out of her own goodness make the net
That shall enmesh them all.

Enter RODERIGO.

How, now, Roderigo!

RODERIGO.

I do follow here in the chase, not like a hound that hunts, but one that fills up the cry.[9] My money is almost spent; I have been to-night exceedingly well cudgell'd; and I think the issue will be—I shall have so much experience for my pains; and so, with no money at all, and a little more wit, return again to Venice.

IAGO.

How poor are they that have not patience!

---

[1] **list:** pleases. [2] **appetite:** wishes. [3] **play the god/With his weak function:** that is, master his weakened mental faculties. [4] **put on:** advance; thrust forward. [5] **suggest:** tempt; seduce. [6] **Plies:** pleads with. [7] **repeals him:** recalls him. [8] **pitch:** blackness; evil. [9] **fills up the cry:** adds to the voice of the hounds to no good purpose.

What wound did ever heal but by degrees?
Thou know'st we work by wit, and not by witchcraft;
And wit depends on dilatory[1] time.
Does't not go well? Cassio hath beaten thee,
And thou, by that small hurt, hast cashier'd Cassio:
Though other things grow fair against the sun,
Yet fruits that blossom first will first be ripe:
Content thyself awhile.—By th'mass, 'tis morning;
Pleasure and action make the hours seem short.—
Retire thee; go where thou art billeted:
Away, I say; thou shalt know more hereafter:
Nay, get thee gone. [*Exit* RODERIGO.] Two things are to be done,—
My wife must move[2] for Cassio to her mistress;
I'll set her on;
Myself the while to draw the Moor apart,
And bring him jump[3] when he may Cassio find
Soliciting his wife:—ay, that's the way;
Dull not device[4] by coldness[5] and delay. [*Exit.*

---

[1] **dilatory:** lagging; tardy.
[2] **move:** intercede; petition.
[3] **jump:** exactly at the moment.
[4] **device:** the plan.
[5] **coldness:** lack of interest.

Othello

ACT 3

ACT III

CASSIO follows Iago's advice the very next morning. He is making his request when Othello and Iago walk in; Cassio leaves in embarrassment. Iago hints distantly at Cassio's silent exit. But this comes to nothing, for Desdemona immediately tells her husband the reason Cassio had come. Iago has to begin his insinuations over again, more circumspectly and elaborately. He speaks of Desdemona's former friendliness with Cassio, of the dangers of unwarranted jealousy, of the duplicity of the sophisticated Venetian wives. After all, Desdemona had deceived her father successfully. And the very strangeness of Desdemona choosing a husband so exotic is in itself suspect. Othello begins to feel the weight of all these hints, all the more in hearing them from a straightforward friend. When Desdemona enters, she notices Othello's upset. Trying to soothe the headache Othello uses as an excuse, she accidentally drops a handkerchief Othello has given her. And this Iago secures. The poison has begun to work in Othello's mind. But his reaction catches even Iago off guard. Othello now demands definite proof of his wife's infidelity at the price of Iago's own life. Othello must choose between a woman he loves entirely and a friend he trusts totally. Iago's manipulation and plotting is now in deadly earnest, for his own life is at stake. His case against Cassio and Desdemona must be quickly and completely established. The necessary basis for it is the rousing of Othello's enormous passion and wrath. Desdemona is puzzled by the change in Othello but cannot account for it, nor for any reason why he should be jealous. Cassio, too, is completely unaware of the plot around him. He has found a colorful handkerchief in his room and gives it to his mistress, Bianca, to make a copy of it for himself.

ACT III. SCENE I.

Cyprus. Before the castle.

Enter CASSIO *and some* MUSICIANS.

CASSIO.

Masters, play here,—I will content your pains,[1]—
Something that's brief; and bid 'Good morrow, general.'

[*Music.*

Enter CLOWN.

CLOWN.

Why, masters, have your instruments been in Naples,[2] that they speak i'th'nose thus?

[1] **content your pains:** that is, reward your efforts.
[2] **have your instruments been in Naples:** this refers either to the nasal tone of the Neapolitans or to the fact that syphilis (prevalent in Naples at this time) might have eaten away the nose.

FIRST MUSICIAN.

How, sir, how!

CLOWN.

Are these, I pray you, wind-instruments?

FIRST MUSICIAN.

Ay, marry, are they, sir.

CLOWN.

O, thereby hangs a tail.

FIRST MUSICIAN.

Whereby hangs a tale, sir?

CLOWN.

Marry, sir, by many a wind-instrument that I know. But, masters, here's money for you: and the general so likes your music, that he desires you, of all loves,[1] to make no more noise with it.

FIRST MUSICIAN.

Well, sir, we will not.

CLOWN.

If you have any music that may not be heard, to't again: but, as they say, to hear music the general does not greatly care.

FIRST MUSICIAN.

We have none such, sir.

CLOWN.

Then put up your pipes in your bag, for I'll away: go; vanish into air; away! [*Exeunt* MUSICIANS.

CASSIO.

Dost thou hear, my honest friend?

CLOWN.

No, I hear not your honest friend; I hear you.

---

[1] of all loves: for love's sake.

CASSIO.

Prithee, keep up thy quillets.[1] There's a poor piece of gold for thee: if the gentlewoman that attends the general's wife be stirring, tell her there's one Cassio entreats her a little favour of speech: wilt thou do this?

CLOWN.

She is stirring, sir: if she will stir hither, I shall seem to notify unto her.[2]

CASSIO.

Do, good my friend. [*Exit* CLOWN.

Enter IAGO.

In happy time,[3] Iago.

IAGO.

You have not been a-bed, then?

CASSIO.

Why, no; the day had broke
Before we parted. I have made bold, Iago,
To send in to your wife: my suit to her
Is, that she will to virtuous Desdemona
Procure me some access.

IAGO.

I'll send her to you presently;[4]
And I'll devise a mean[5] to draw the Moor
Out of the way, that your converse and business
May be more free.

CASSIO.

I humbly thank you for't. [*Exit* IAGO.] I never knew
A Florentine more kind and honest.

---

[1] **keep up thy quillets:** keep your puns to yourself.
[2] **seem to notify unto her:** tell her (the Clown is trying to imitate Cassio's way of speaking).
[3] **In happy time:** that is, we have met at an opportune moment.
[4] **presently:** at once.
[5] **a mean:** some means.

Enter EMILIA.

EMILIA.

Good morrow, good lieutenant: I am sorry
For your displeasure;[1] but all will sure be well.
The general and his wife are talking of it;
And she speaks for you stoutly: the Moor replies,
That he you hurt is of great fame in Cyprus
And great affinity,[2] and that in wholesome wisdom[3]
He might not but refuse you; but he protests he loves you,
And needs no other suitor but his likings
To take the safest occasion by the front
To bring you in again.[4]

CASSIO.

Yet, I beseech you,—
If you think fit, or that it may be done,—
Give me advantage of some brief discourse
With Desdemona alone.

EMILIA.

Pray you, come in:
I will bestow[5] you where you shall have time
To speak your bosom freely.[6]

CASSIO.

I am much bound to you. [*Exeunt.*

SCENE II.

A room in the castle.

Enter OTHELLO, IAGO, *and* GENTLEMEN.

OTHELLO.

These letters give, Iago, to the pilot;
And, by him, do my duties to the senate:
That done, I will be walking on the works;[7]

---

[1] **your displeasure:** the displeasure you have incurred from Othello. [2] **affinity:** family (well-connected). [3] **in wholesome wisdom:** for his own good. [4] **bring you in again:** reinstate you in his favor. [5] **bestow:** quarter. [6] **speak your bosom freely:** speak freely of what is in your heart. [7] **works:** ramparts.

Repair there to me.

IAGO.

Well, my good lord, I'll do't.

OTHELLO.

This fortification, gentlemen,—shall we see't?

GENTLEMAN.

We'll wait upon your lordship. [*Exeunt.*

SCENE III.

The garden of the castle.

Enter DESDEMONA, CASSIO, *and* EMILIA.

DESDEMONA.

Be thou assured, good Cassio, I will do[1]
All my abilities in thy behalf.

EMILIA.

Good madam, do: I warrant it grieves my husband,
As if the case were his.

DESDEMONA.

O, that's an honest fellow.—Do not doubt, Cassio,
But I will have my lord and you again
As friendly as you were.

CASSIO.

Bounteous madam,
Whatever shall become of Michael Cassio,
He's never any thing but your true servant.

DESDEMONA.

I know't,—I thank you. You do love my lord:
You have known him long; and be you well assured

---

[1] do: use.

He shall in strangeness stand no further off
Than in a politic distance.[1]

CASSIO.

Ay, but, lady,
That policy may either last so long,
Or feed upon such nice and waterish diet,[2]
Or breed itself so out of circumstance,[3]
That, I being absent, and my place supplied,
My general will forget my love and service.

DESDEMONA.

Do not doubt that; before Emilia here
I give thee warrant of thy place: assure thee,
If I do vow a friendship, I'll perform it
To the last article: my lord shall never rest;
I'll watch him tame,[4] and talk him out of patience;
His bed shall seem a school, his board a shrift;[5]
I'll intermingle every thing he does
With Cassio's suit: therefore be merry, Cassio;
For thy solicitor shall rather die
Than give thy cause away.[6]

EMILIA.

Madam, here comes my lord.

CASSIO.

Madam, I'll take my leave.

DESDEMONA.

Why, stay, and hear me speak.

CASSIO.

Madam, not now: I am very ill at ease,
Unfit for mine own purposes.

DESDEMONA.

Well, do your discretion. [*Exit* CASSIO.

Enter OTHELLO *and* IAGO.

---

[1] **He shall . . . distance:** He shall be no more aloof than discretion warrants. [2] **feed upon such nice and waterish diet:** that is, be motivated by such trivial and weak considerations. [3] **breed . . . circumstance:** grow stronger because of unforeseen circumstances. [4] **watch him tame:** keep him awake day and night (as in taming wild hawks). [5] **a shrift:** a confessional. [6] **give thy cause away:** abandon your cause.

IAGO.

Ha! I like not that.

OTHELLO.

What dost thou say?

IAGO.

Nothing, my lord: or if—I know not what.

OTHELLO.

Was not that Cassio parted from my wife?

IAGO.

Cassio, my lord! No, sure, I cannot think it,
That he would steal away so guilty-like,
Seeing you coming.

OTHELLO.

I do believe 'twas he.

DESDEMONA.

How now, my lord!
I have been talking with a suitor here,
A man that languishes in your displeasure.

OTHELLO.

Who is't you mean?

DESDEMONA.

Why, your lieutenant, Cassio. Good my lord,
If I have any grace or power to move you,
His present reconciliation take;
For if he be not one that truly loves you,
That errs in ignorance, and not in cunning,[1]
I have no judgement in an honest face:
I prithee, call him back.

OTHELLO.

Went he hence now?

DESDEMONA.

Ay, sooth;[2] so humbled,
That he hath left part of his grief with me,
To suffer with him. Good love, call him back.

---

[1] **cunning:** knowledge.
[2] **sooth:** in truth.

OTHELLO.

Not now, sweet Desdemona; some other time.

DESDEMONA.

But shall't be shortly?

OTHELLO.

The sooner, sweet, for you.

DESDEMONA.

Shall't be to-night at supper?

OTHELLO.

No, not to-night.

DESDEMONA.

To-morrow dinner, then?

OTHELLO.

I shall not dine at home;
I meet the captains at the citadel.

DESDEMONA.

Why, then, to-morrow night; or Tuesday morn;
On Tuesday noon, or night; on Wednesday morn:—
I prithee, name the time; but let it not
Exceed three days: in faith, he's penitent;
And yet his trespass, in our common reason,[1]—
Save that, they say, the wars must make examples
Out of their best,—is not almost a fault
T'incur a private check.[2] When shall he come?
Tell me, Othello: I wonder in my soul,
What you would ask me, that I should deny,
Or stand so mammering on.[3] What! Michael Cassio,
That came a-wooing with you; and so many a time,
When I have spoke of you dispraisingly,
Hath ta'en your part; to have so much to do
To bring him in! Trust me, I could do much—

---

[1] in our common reason: as we judge such things.
[2] check: rebuke.
[3] so mammering on: in so much hesitation about.

OTHELLO.

Prithee, no more: let him come when he will;
I will deny thee nothing.

DESDEMONA.

Why, this is not a boon;
'Tis as I should entreat you wear your gloves,
Or feed on nourishing dishes, or keep you warm,
Or sue to you to do a peculiar profit[1]
To your own person: nay, when I have a suit
Wherein I mean to touch your love indeed,
It shall be full of poise[2] and difficult weight,
And fearful [3] to be granted.

OTHELLO.

I will deny thee nothing:
Whereon, I do beseech thee, grant me this,
To leave me but a little to myself.

DESDEMONA.

Shall I deny you? no: farewell, my lord.

OTHELLO.

Farewell, my Desdemona: I'll come to thee straight.[4]

DESDEMONA.

Emilia, come.—Be as your fancies teach you;
Whate'er you be, I am obedient. [*Exit, with* EMILIA.

OTHELLO.

Excellent wretch! [5] Perdition catch my soul,
But I do love thee! and when I love thee not,
Chaos is come again.

IAGO.

My noble lord,—

OTHELLO.

What dost thou say, Iago?

---

[1] **a peculiar profit:** that is, something particularly advantageous.
[2] **poise:** weight; importance.
[3] **fearful:** involving fear or danger.
[4] **straight:** at once; immediately.
[5] **wretch:** a term of endearment in this case.

IAGO.

Did Michael Cassio, when you woo'd my lady,
Know of your love?

OTHELLO.

He did, from first to last: why dost thou ask?

IAGO.

But for a satisfaction of my thought;
No further harm.

OTHELLO.

Why of thy thought, Iago?

IAGO.

I did not think he had been acquainted with her.

OTHELLO.

O, yes; and went between us[1] very oft.

IAGO.

Indeed!

OTHELLO.

Indeed! ay, indeed:—discern'st thou aught in that?
Is he not honest?

IAGO.

Honest, my lord!

OTHELLO.

Honest! ay, honest.

IAGO.

My lord, for aught I know.

OTHELLO.

What dost thou think?

IAGO.

Think, my lord!

OTHELLO.

Think, my lord!

By heaven, he echoes me,

---

[1] **went between us:** acted as an emissary during our courtship.

As if there were some monster in his thought
Too hideous to be shown.—Thou dost mean something:
I heard thee say even now, thou likedst not that,
When Cassio left my wife: what didst not like?
And when I told thee he was of my counsel [1]
In my whole course of wooing, thou criedst 'Indeed!'
And didst contract and purse thy brow together,
As if thou then hadst shut up in thy brain
Some horrible conceit: [2] if thou dost love me,
Show me thy thought.

IAGO.

My lord, you know I love you.

OTHELLO.

I think thou dost;
And, for I know thou'rt full of love and honesty,
And weigh'st thy words before thou givest them breath,
Therefore these stops [3] of thine fright me the more:
For such things in a false disloyal knave
Are tricks of custom, [4] but in a man that's just
They're close delations, [5] working from the heart,
That passion cannot rule.

IAGO.

For Michael Cassio,
I dare be sworn I think that he is honest.

OTHELLO.

I think so too.

IAGO.

Men should be what they seem;
Or those that be not, would they might seem none! [6]

---

[1] **of my counsel:** in my confidence.
[2] **conceit:** thought.
[3] **stops:** hesitations; pauses.
[4] **tricks of custom:** tricks of their trade.
[5] **close delations:** secret accusations.
[6] **might seem none:** might not resemble men.

OTHELLO.

Certain, men should be what they seem.

IAGO.

Why, then, I think Cassio's an honest man.

OTHELLO.

Nay, yet there's more in this:
I prithee, speak to me as to thy thinkings,
As thou dost ruminate; and give thy worst of thoughts
The worst of words.

IAGO.

Good my lord, pardon me:
Though I am bound to every act of duty,
I am not bound to that all slaves are free to.[1]
Utter my thoughts? Why, say they are vile and false,—
As where's that palace whereinto foul things
Sometimes intrude not? who has a breast so pure,
But some uncleanly apprehensions
Keep leets and law-days,[2] and in session sit
With meditations lawful?

OTHELLO.

Thou dost conspire against thy friend, Iago,
If thou but think'st him wrong'd, and makest his ear
A stranger to thy thoughts.

IAGO.

I do beseech you—
Though I perchance am vicious in my guess,[3]
As, I confess, it is my nature's plague
To spy into abuses,[4] and oft my jealousy[5]
Shapes faults that are not—that your wisdom yet,
From one that so imperfectly conceits,[6]

---

[1] **I am not bound to that all slaves are free to:** I am not obligated to reveal my secret thoughts, a right enjoyed even by slaves. [2] **leets and law-days:** meetings of local courts (*leets* and *law-days* are synonymous). [3] **vicious in my guess:** overly suspicious. [4] **abuses:** deceptions. [5] **jealousy:** suspicious nature. [6] **conceits:** imagines; conceives.

Would take no notice; nor build yourself a trouble
Out of his scattering[1] and unsure observance:—
It were not for your quiet[2] nor your good,
Nor for my manhood, honesty, or wisdom,
To let you know my thoughts.

OTHELLO.

What dost thou mean?

IAGO.

Good name in man and woman, dear my lord,
Is the immediate[3] jewel of their souls:
Who steals my purse steals trash; 'tis something, nothing;
'Twas mine, 'tis his, and has been slave to thousands;
But he that filches from me my good name
Robs me of that which not enriches him,
And makes me poor indeed.

OTHELLO.

By heaven, I'll know thy thoughts!

IAGO.

You cannot, if my heart were in your hand;
Nor shall not, whilst 'tis in my custody.

OTHELLO.

Ha!

IAGO.

O, beware, my lord, of jealousy;
It is the green-eyed monster, which doth mock
The meat it feeds on: that cuckold lives in bliss
Who, certain of his fate, loves not his wronger;
But, O, what damned minutes tells he o'er
Who dotes, yet doubts, suspects, yet strongly loves!

OTHELLO.

O misery!

---

[1] **scattering:** random.
[2] **It were not for your quiet:** it would not be conducive to your peace of mind.
[3] **immediate:** most precious; nearest to the heart.

IAGO.

Poor and content is rich, and rich enough;
But riches fineless[1] is as poor as winter
To him that ever fears he shall be poor:—
Good heaven, the souls of all my tribe defend
From jealousy!

OTHELLO.

Why, why is this?
Think'st thou I'ld make a life of jealousy,
To follow still [2] the changes of the moon
With fresh suspicions? No; to be once in doubt
Is once to be resolved:[3] exchange me for a goat,
When I shall turn the business of my soul
To such exsufflicate[4] and blown[5] surmises,
Matching thy inference. 'Tis not to make me jealous
To say my wife is fair, feeds well, loves company,
Is free of speech, sings, plays, and dances well;
Where virtue is, these are more virtuous:
Nor from mine own weak merits will I draw
The smallest fear or doubt of her revolt;[6]
For she had eyes, and chose me. No, Iago;
I'll see before I doubt; when I doubt, prove;
And, on the proof, there is no more but this,—
Away at once with love or jealousy!

IAGO.

I am glad of it; for now I shall have reason
To show the love and duty that I bear you
With franker spirit: therefore, as I am bound,
Receive it from me:—I speak not yet of proof.
Look to your wife; observe her well with Cassio;
Wear your eye thus, not jealous[7] nor secure:[8]
I would not have your free and noble nature,

---

[1] **fineless:** unbounded; infinite. [2] **still:** always. [3] **resolved:** determined to track down the truth. [4] **exsufficate:** exaggerated; puffed out. [5] **blown:** flyblown. [6] **revolt:** desertion. [7] **jealous:** suspicious. [8] **secure:** completely trustful.

Out of self-bounty,[1] be abused;[2] look to't:
I know our country disposition well;
In Venice they do let heaven see the pranks
They dare not show their husbands; their best conscience
Is—not to leave undone, but keep unknown.

OTHELLO.

Dost thou say so?

IAGO.

She did deceive her father, marrying you;
And when she seem'd to shake and fear your looks,
She loved them most.

OTHELLO.

And so she did.

IAGO.

Why, go to, then;[3]
She that, so young, could give out such a seeming,[4]
To seel [5] her father's eyes up close as oak[6]—
He thought 'twas witchcraft:—but I am much to blame;
I humbly do beseech you of your pardon
For too much loving you.

OTHELLO.

I am bound to thee for ever.

IAGO.

I see this hath a little dasht your spirits.

OTHELLO.

Not a jot, not a jot.

IAGO.

I'faith, I fear it has.
I hope you will consider what is spoke
Comes from my love;—but I do see y'are moved:[7]—

---

[1] **self-bounty:** innate generosity. [2] **abused:** deceived. [3] **Why, go to, then:** why, there you are. [4] **a seeming:** an appearance. [5] **seel:** hoodwink (a term in falconry). [6] **close as oak:** many think that *oak* is a misprint here; however, oak is one of the most close-grained of all woods. [7] **moved:** visibly affected; excited.

I am to pray you not to strain my speech
To grosser issues[1] nor to larger reach
Than to suspicion.

OTHELLO.

I will not.

IAGO.

Should you do so, my lord,
My speech should fall into such vile success[2]
As my thoughts aim not at. Cassio's my worthy friend:—
My lord, I see y'are moved.

OTHELLO.

No, not much moved:—
I do not think but Desdemona's honest.[3]

IAGO.

Long live she so! and long live you to think so!

OTHELLO.

And yet, how nature erring from itself,—

IAGO.

Ay, there's the point:—as—to be bold with you—
Not to affect[4] many proposed matches
Of her own clime, complexion,[5] and degree,
Whereto we see in all things nature tends,—
Foh! one may smell in such, a will most rank,[6]
Foul disproportion,[7] thoughts unnatural:—
But pardon me: I do not in position
Distinctly speak of her; though I may fear
Her will, recoiling to[8] her better judgement,
May fall to match you with her country forms,[9]
And happily[10] repent.

OTHELLO.

Farewell, farewell:
If more thou dost perceive, let me know more;

---

[1] **grosser issues:** greater conclusions. [2] **success:** consequences. [3] **honest:** faithful. [4] **to affect:** to be inclined toward. [5] **complexion:** temperament. [6] **a will most rank:** desires most foul. [7] **disproportion:** disharmony. [8] **recoiling to:** spurning. [9] **May fall to match you with her country forms:** may happen to compare you with her countrymen. [10] **happily:** perchance.

Set on thy wife to observe: leave me, Iago.

IAGO.

My lord, I take my leave. [*Going.*

OTHELLO.

Why did I marry?—This honest creature doubtless
Sees and knows more, much more, than he unfolds.

IAGO [*Returning.*]

My lord, I would I might entreat your honour
To scan[1] this thing no further; leave it to time:
Although 'tis fit that Cassio have his place,—
For, sure, he fills it up with great ability,—
Yet, if you please to hold him off awhile,
You shall by that perceive him and his means:[2]
Note if your lady strain his entertainment[3]
With any strong or vehement importunity;
Much will be seen in that. In the mean time
Let me be thought too busy in my fears,—
As worthy cause I have to fear I am,—
And hold her free,[4] I do beseech your honour.

OTHELLO.

Fear not my government.[5]

IAGO.

I once more take my leave. [*Exit.*

OTHELLO.

This fellow's of exceeding honesty,
And knows all qualities, with a learned spirit,
Of human dealings. If I do prove her haggard,[6]
Though that her jesses[7] were my dear heartstrings,
I'ld whistle her off, and let her down the wind,[8]

---

[1] **scan:** scrutinize. [2] **his means:** his method of soliciting Desdemona's aid. [3] **strain his entertainment:** press hard for his reinstatement. [4] **free:** innocent. [5] **government:** self-control. [6] **haggard:** a mature hawk partly trained for falconry that has reverted to its wild state. [7] **jesses:** leather straps fastened to each leg of a hawk. [8] **whistle her off, and let her down the wind:** release or cast her off; with the wind against her, the hawk must shift for herself.

To prey at fortune. Haply, for I am black,[1]
And have not those soft parts[2] of conversation
That chamberers[3] have; or, for I am declined
Into the vale of years,—yet that's not much;—
She's gone; I am abused; and my relief
Must be to loathe her. O curse of marriage,
That we can call these delicate creatures ours,
And not their appetites! I had rather be a toad,
And live upon the vapour of a dungeon,
Than keep a corner in the thing I love
For others' uses. Yet, 'tis the plague of great ones;
Prerogatived are they less than the base;[4]
'Tis destiny unshunnable, like death:
Even then this forked plague[5] is fated to us
When we do quicken.[6]—Desdemona comes:
If she be false, O, then heaven mocks itself!—
I'll not believe't.

Enter DESDEMONA *and* EMILIA.

DESDEMONA.

How now, my dear Othello!
Your dinner, and the generous islanders[7]
By you invited, do attend your presence.

OTHELLO.

I am to blame.

DESDEMONA.

Why do you speak so faintly?
Are you not well?

OTHELLO.

I have a pain upon my forehead here.

DESDEMONA.

Faith, that's with watching;[8] 'twill away again:
Let me but bind it hard, within this hour
It will be well.

---

[1] **Haply, for I am black:** perhaps because I am black. [2] **parts:** qualities. [3] **chamberers:** courtiers; ladies' men. [4] **Prerogatived are they less than the base:** they are less immune than the lowly. [5] **forked plague:** the horns of the cuckold. [6] **When we do quicken:** when we are born. [7] **generous islanders:** the most high-ranking islanders. [8] **watching:** wakefulness.

OTHELLO.

Your napkin[1] is too little;

[*He puts the handkerchief from him; and she drops it.*

Let it alone. Come, I'll go in with you.

DESDEMONA.

I am very sorry that you are not well.

[*Exeunt* OTHELLO *and* DESDEMONA.

EMILIA.

I am glad I have found this napkin:
This was her first remembrance from the Moor:
My wayward husband hath a hundred times
Woo'd me to steal it; but she so loves the token,—
For he conjured her she should ever keep it,—
That she reserves it evermore about her
To kiss and talk to. I'll have the work ta'en out,[2]
And give't Iago:
What he will do with it heaven knows, not I;
I nothing but to please his fantasy.

Enter IAGO.

IAGO.

How now! what do you here alone?

EMILIA.

Do not you chide; I have a thing for you.

IAGO.

A thing for me!—it is a common thing—

EMILIA.

Ha!

IAGO.

To have a foolish wife.

EMILIA.

O, is that all? What will you give me now
For that same handkerchief?

---

[1] **napkin:** handkerchief.

[2] **I'll have the work ta'en out:** I'll have the embroidered design copied (on another handkerchief).

IAGO.

What handkerchief?

EMILIA.

What handkerchief!
Why, that the Moor first gave to Desdemona;
That which so often you did bid me steal.

IAGO.

Hast stoln it from her?

EMILIA.

No, faith; she let it drop by negligence,
And, to th'advantage,[1] I, being here, took't up.
Look, here it is.

IAGO.

A good wench; give it me.

EMILIA.

What will you do with't, that you have been so earnest
To have me filch it?

IAGO.

Why, what's that to you? [*Snatching it.*

EMILIA.

If't be not for some purpose of import,[2]
Give't me again: poor lady, she'll run mad
When she shall lack[3] it.

IAGO.

Be not acknown on't;[4] I have use for it.
Go, leave me. [*Exit* EMILIA.
I will in Cassio's lodging lose this napkin,
And let him find it. Trifles light as air
Are to the jealous confirmations strong
As proofs of holy writ: this may do something.
The Moor already changes with my poison:—
Dangerous conceits[5] are, in their natures, poisons,

---

[1] to th'advantage: luckily.
[2] import: importance.
[3] lack: miss.
[4] Be not acknown on't: do not acknowledge knowing anything about it.
[5] conceits: thoughts; imaginings.

Which at the first are scarce found to distaste,[1]
But, with a little act upon the blood,[2]
Burn like the mines of sulphur.—I did say so:—
Look, where he comes! Not poppy, nor mandragora,[3]
Nor all the drowsy syrups of the world,
Shall ever medicine thee to that sweet sleep
Which thou owedst[4] yesterday.

Enter OTHELLO.

OTHELLO.

Ha! ha! false to me?

IAGO.

Why, how now, general! no more of that.

OTHELLO.

Avaunt! be gone! thou hast set me on the rack:—
I swear 'tis better to be much abused
Than but to know't a little.

IAGO.

How now, my lord!

OTHELLO.

What sense had I of her stoln hours of lust?
I saw't not, thought it not, it harm'd not me:
I slept the next night well, was free and merry;
I found not Cassio's kisses on her lips:
He that is robb'd, not wanting[5] what is stoln,
Let him not know't, and he's not robb'd at all.

IAGO.

I am sorry to hear this.

OTHELLO.

I had been happy, if the general camp,
Pioners[6] and all, had tasted her sweet body,
So I had nothing known. O, now, for ever
Farewell the tranquil mind! farewell content!

---

[1] **distaste:** taste bad. [2] **with a little act upon the blood:** that is, within a short period of time. [3] **mandragora:** an herb plant that induced healing sleep. [4] **owedst:** owned; possessed. [5] **wanting:** missing. [6] **Pioners:** the lowliest of all soldiers, who dug trenches and performed other menial duties.

Farewell the plumed troop, and the big wars,
That make ambition virtue! O, farewell!
Farewell the neighing steed, and the shrill trump,[1]
The spirit-stirring drum, th'ear-piercing fife,
The royal banner, and all quality,
Pride, pomp, and circumstance[2] of glorious war!
And, O you mortal engines,[3] whose rude throats
Th'immortal Jove's dread clamours counterfeit,
Farewell! Othello's occupation's gone!

IAGO.

Is't possible, my lord?

OTHELLO.

Villain, be sure thou prove my love a whore,—
Be sure of it; give me the ocular proof;
Or, by the worth of man's eternal soul,
Thou hadst been better have been born a dog
Than answer my waked wrath!

IAGO.

Is't come to this?

OTHELLO.

Make me to see't; or, at the least, so prove it,
That the probation[4] bear no hinge nor loop
To hang a doubt on; or woe upon thy life!

IAGO.

My noble lord,—

OTHELLO.

If thou dost slander her, and torture me,
Never pray more; abandon all remorse;[5]
On horror's head horrors accumulate;
Do deeds to make heaven weep, all earth amazed;
For nothing canst thou to damnation add
Greater than that.

---

[1] **trump:** trumpet.
[2] **circumstance:** pageantry.
[3] **mortal engines:** deadly machines (cannon).
[4] **probation:** proof.
[5] **all remorse:** all tenderness or pity; conscience.

IAGO.

O grace! O heaven forgive me!
Are you a man? have you a soul or sense?—
God be wi'you! take mine office.—O wretched fool,
That livest to make thine honesty a vice!—
O monstrous world! Take note, take note, O world,
To be direct and honest is not safe.—
I thank you for this profit;[1] and from hence
I'll love no friend, sith[2] love breeds such offence.

OTHELLO.

Nay, stay:—thou shouldst be honest.

IAGO.

I should be wise; for honesty's a fool,
And loses that it works for.[3]

OTHELLO.

By the world,
I think my wife be honest, and think she is not;
I think that thou art just, and think thou art not:
I'll have some proof: her name, that was as fresh
As Dian's[4] visage, is now begrimed and black
As mine own face.—If there be cords or knives,
Poison, or fire, or suffocating streams,[5]
I'll not endure it.—Would I were satisfied!

IAGO.

I see, sir, you are eaten up with passion:
I do repent me that I put it to you.
You would be satisfied?

OTHELLO.

Would! nay, I will.

IAGO.

And may: but, how? how satisfied, my lord?
Would you, the supervisor,[6] grossly gape on,[7]—
Behold her topt?

---

[1] **profit:** profitable lesson. [2] **sith:** with the meaning of since, but used by Shakespeare with logic, while *since* is used with time. [3] **loses that it works for:** loses the trust that honesty calls for. [4] **Dian:** Diana—goddess of the moon and symbol of chastity. [5] **cords or knives . . . streams:** all means of committing suicide. [6] **supervisor:** onlooker. [7] **grossly gape on:** rudely spy on her.

OTHELLO.

Death and damnation! O!

IAGO.

It were a tedious difficulty, I think,
To bring them to that prospect: damn them, then,
If ever mortal eyes do see them bolster[1]
More than their own! What then? how then?
What shall I say? Where's satisfaction?
It is impossible you should see this,
Were they as prime[2] as goats, as hot as monkeys,
As salt[3] as wolves in pride,[4] and fools as gross
As ignorance made drunk. But yet, I say,
If imputation and strong circumstances[5]—
Which lead directly to the door of truth—
Will give you satisfaction, you may have't.

OTHELLO.

Give me a living reason[6] she's disloyal.

IAGO.

I do not like the office:
But, sith I am enter'd in this cause so far,—
Prickt to't[7] by foolish honesty and love,—
I will go on. I lay with Cassio lately;
And, being troubled with a raging tooth,
I could not sleep.
There are a kind of men so loose of soul
That in their sleeps will mutter their affairs;
One of this kind is Cassio:
In sleep I heard him say, 'Sweet Desdemona,
Let us be wary, let us hide our loves;'
And then, sir, would he gripe and wring my hand,
Cry 'O sweet creature!' and then kiss me hard,
As if he pluckt up kisses by the roots
That grew upon my lips: then laid his leg

---

[1] **bolster:** go to bed with. [2] **prime:** lustful. [3] **salt:** lecherous. [4] **pride:** heat. [5] **strong circumstances:** weighty evidence. [6] **living reason:** that is, reason founded on fact, not conjecture. [7] **Prickt to't:** spurred on.

Over my thigh, and sigh'd, and kist; and then
Cried 'Cursed fate that gave thee to the Moor!'

OTHELLO.

O monstrous! monstrous!

IAGO.

Nay, this was but his dream.

OTHELLO.

But this denoted a foregone conclusion:[1]
'Tis a shrewd doubt,[2] though it be but a dream.

IAGO.

And this may help to thicken other proofs
That do demonstrate thinly.

OTHELLO.

I'll tear her all to pieces.

IAGO.

Nay, but be wise: yet we see nothing done;
She may be honest yet. Tell me but this,—
Have you not sometimes seen a handkerchief
Spotted with strawberries in your wife's hand?

OTHELLO.

I gave her such a one; 'twas my first gift.

IAGO.

I know not that: but such a handkerchief—
I am sure it was your wife's—did I to-day
See Cassio wipe his beard with.

OTHELLO.

If it be that,—

IAGO.

If it be that, or any that was hers,
It speaks against her with the other proofs.

OTHELLO.

O, that the slave had forty thousand lives,—
One is too poor, too weak for my revenge!

---

[1] **a foregone conclusion:** something that had already taken place.
[2] **shrewd doubt:** suspicion based on truth.

Now do I see 'tis true.—Look here, Iago;
All my fond love thus do I blow to heaven:
'Tis gone.—
Arise, black vengeance, from the hollow hell!
Yield up, O love, thy crown and hearted throne
To tyrannous hate! Swell, bosom, with thy fraught,[1]
For 'tis of aspics' tongues! [2]

IAGO.

Yet be content.[3]

OTHELLO.

O, blood, blood, blood!

IAGO.

Patience, I say; your mind perhaps may change.

OTHELLO.

Never, Iago. Like to the Pontic sea,[4]
Whose icy current and compulsive course
Ne'er feels retiring ebb, but keeps due on
To the Propontic[5] and the Hellespont;[6]
Even so my bloody thoughts, with violent pace,
Shall ne'er look back, ne'er ebb to humble love,
Till that a capable and wide revenge
Swallow them up.—Now, by yond marble heaven,[7]
In the due reverence of a sacred vow [*Kneels.*
I here engage[8] my words.

IAGO.

Do not rise yet.— [*Kneels.*
Witness, you ever-burning lights above,
You elements that clip[9] us round about,—
Witness that here Iago doth give up
The execution[10] of his wit, hands, heart,
To wrong'd Othello's service! Let him command,
And to obey shall be in me remorse,[11]

---

[1] **fraught:** burden. [2] **aspics' tongues:** asps' tongues. [3] **Yet be content:** in spite of this, remain calm. [4] **Pontic sea:** the Black Sea. [5] **Propontic:** Sea of Marmora. [6] **Hellespont:** a strait connecting the Sea of Marmora with the Black Sea. [7] **marble heaven:** a cloud-streaked sky. [8] **engage:** pledge. [9] **clip:** embrace. [10] **execution:** employment. [11] **to obey shall be in me remorse:** to carry out your command will be done in a spirit of pity.

What bloody business ever. [*They rise.*

OTHELLO.

I greet[1] thy love,
Not with vain thanks, but with acceptance bounteous,
And will upon the instant put thee to't:
Within these three days let me hear thee say
That Cassio's not alive.

IAGO.

My friend is dead; 'tis done at your request:
But let her live.

OTHELLO.

Damn her, lewd minx! O, damn her!
Come, go with me apart; I will withdraw,
To furnish me with some swift means of death
For the fair devil. Now art thou my lieutenant.

IAGO.

I am your own for ever. [*Exeunt.*

Scene IV.

Before the castle.

Enter DESDEMONA, EMILIA, *and* CLOWN.

DESDEMONA.

Do you know, sirrah, where Lieutenant Cassio lies? [2]

CLOWN.

I dare not say he lies any where.

DESDEMONA.

Why, man?

CLOWN.

He's a soldier; and for one to say a soldier lies, is stabbing.[3]

---

[1] **greet:** welcome.
[2] **lies:** lodges.
[3] **is stabbing:** that is, the person saying it is in danger of being stabbed.

DESDEMONA.

Go to: where lodges he?

CLOWN.

To tell you where he lodges, is to tell you where I lie.

DESDEMONA.

Can any thing be made of this?

CLOWN.

I know not where he lodges; and for me to devise a lodging, and say he lies here or he lies there, were to lie in mine own throat.[1]

DESDEMONA.

Can you inquire him out, and be edified [2] by report?

CLOWN.

I will catechize the world for him; that is, make questions, and by them answer.

DESDEMONA.

Seek him, bid him come hither: tell him I have moved my lord on his behalf, and hope all will be well.

CLOWN.

To do this is within the compass of man's wit; and therefore I will attempt the doing it. [*Exit.*

DESDEMONA.

Where should I lose that handkerchief, Emilia?

EMILIA.

I know not, madam.

DESDEMONA.

Believe me, I had rather have lost my purse
Full of crusadoes:[3] and, but[4] my noble Moor
Is true of mind, and made of no such baseness
As jealous creatures are, it were enough
To put him to ill thinking.

---

[1] **were to lie in my own throat:** i.e., would be to lie wilfully.
[2] **edified:** enlightened (Desdemona is imitating the Clown's exaggerated way of talking).
[3] **crusadoes:** Portuguese coins, so called because of the cross stamped on them.
[4] **but:** but that.

EMILIA.

Is he not jealous?

DESDEMONA.

Who, he? I think the sun where he was born
Drew all such humours[1] from him.

EMILIA.

Look, where he comes.

DESDEMONA.

I will not leave him now till Cassio
Be call'd to him.

Enter OTHELLO.

How is't with you, my lord?

OTHELLO.

Well, my good lady.—[*aside*] O, hardness to dissemble! [2]—
How do you, Desdemona?

DESDEMONA.

Well, my good lord.

OTHELLO.

Give me your hand: this hand is moist, my lady.

DESDEMONA.

It yet hath felt no age nor known no sorrow.

OTHELLO.

This argues fruitfulness[3] and liberal [4] heart:—
Hot, hot, and moist: this hand of yours requires
A sequester[5] from liberty, fasting and prayer,
Much castigation[6] exercise devout;[7]
For here's a young and sweating devil here,
That commonly rebels. 'Tis a good hand,
A frank one.

DESDEMONA.

You may, indeed, say so;
For 'twas that hand that gave away my heart.

---

[1] **humours:** characteristics; qualities. [2] **hardness to dissemble:** how hard it is to dissemble. [3] **fruitfulness:** a bountiful nature. [4] **liberal:** free (licentious). [5] **sequester:** withdrawal. [6] **castigation:** chastisement. [7] **exercise devout:** strict attention to religious duties.

OTHELLO.

A liberal hand: the hearts of old gave hands;
But our new heraldry is hands, not hearts.[1]

DESDEMONA.

I cannot speak of this. Come now, your promise.

OTHELLO.

What promise, chuck? [2]

DESDEMONA.

I have sent to bid Cassio come speak with you.

OTHELLO.

I have a salt and sorry rheum[3] offends me;
Lend me thy handkerchief.

DESDEMONA.

Here, my lord.

OTHELLO.

That which I gave you.

DESDEMONA.

I have it not about me.

OTHELLO.

Not?

DESDEMONA.

No, indeed, my lord.

OTHELLO.

That is a fault.

That handkerchief
Did an Egyptian[4] to my mother give;
She was a charmer,[5] and could almost read
The thoughts of people: she told her, while she kept it,
'Twould make her amiable[6] and subdue my father
Entirely to her love; but if she lost it,
Or made a gift of it, my father's eye
Should hold her loathed, and his spirits should hunt
After new fancies: she, dying, gave it me;

---

[1] **But our new heraldry is hands, not hearts:** that is, the fashion or practice now is to give the hand in marriage without consulting the heart. [2] **chuck:** chick (a term of endearment). [3] **a salt and sorry rheum:** a runny, miserable head cold. [4] **Egyptian:** Shakespeare might have meant *gypsy*. [5] **charmer:** fortune teller. [6] **amiable:** lovable; desirable.

And bid me, when my fate would have me wive,
To give it her. I did so: and take heed on't;
Make it a darling like your precious eye;
To lose't or give't away were such perdition[1]
As nothing else could match.

DESDEMONA.

Is't possible?

OTHELLO.

'Tis true: there's magic in the web of it:
A sibyl,[2] that had number'd in the world
The sun to course two hundred compasses,[3]
In her prophetic fury sew'd the work;
The worms were hallow'd that did breed the silk;
And it was dyed in mummy[4] which the skilful
Conserved [5] of maidens' hearts.

DESDEMONA.

Indeed! is't true?

OTHELLO.

Most veritable; therefore look to't well.

DESDEMONA.

Then would to God that I had never seen't!

OTHELLO.

Ha! wherefore?

DESDEMONA.

Why do you speak so startingly[6] and rash?

OTHELLO.

Is't lost? is't gone? speak; is't out o'the way?

DESDEMONA.

Heaven bless us!

OTHELLO.

Say you?

DESDEMONA.

It is not lost; but what an if it were?

---

[1] perdition: loss. [2] sibyl: fortune teller. [3] The sun to course two hundred compasses: that is, she was two hundred years old. [4] mummy: the liquid from embalmed bodies, supposed to have magical properties. [5] Conserved: preserved. [6] startingly: abruptly; excitedly.

OTHELLO.

How!

DESDEMONA.

I say, it is not lost.

OTHELLO.

Fetch't, let me see't.

DESDEMONA.

Why, so I can, sir, but I will not now.
This is a trick to put me from my suit:
Pray you, let Cassio be received again.

OTHELLO.

Fetch me the handkerchief: my mind misgives.[1]

DESDEMONA.

Come, come;
You'll never meet a more sufficient[2] man.

OTHELLO.

The handkerchief!

DESDEMONA.

I pray, talk me of Cassio.

OTHELLO.

The handkerchief!

DESDEMONA.

A man that all his time
Hath founded his good fortunes on your love,
Shared dangers with you,—

OTHELLO.

The handkerchief!

DESDEMONA.

In sooth,[3] you are to blame.

OTHELLO.

Away! [*Exit.*

EMILIA.

Is not this man jealous?

---

[1] **my mind misgives:** my mind is suspicious of this.
[2] **sufficient:** capable (with all the desirable qualities).
[3] **In sooth:** in truth.

DESDEMONA.
I ne'er saw this before.
Sure, there's some wonder in this handkerchief:
I am most unhappy in the loss of it.

EMILIA.
'Tis not a year or two shows us a man:
They are all but stomachs, and we all but food;
They eat us hungerly,[1] and when they are full,
They belch us.—Look you,—Cassio and my husband.

Enter CASSIO *and* IAGO.

IAGO.
There is no other way; 'tis she must do't:
And, lo, the happiness! [2] go, and importune her.

DESDEMONA.
How now, good Cassio! what's the news with you?

CASSIO.
Madam, my former suit: I do beseech you
That by your virtuous means I may again
Exist, and be a member of his love
Whom I with all the office[3] of my heart
Entirely honour: I would not be delay'd.
If my offence be of such mortal kind
That nor my service past, nor present sorrows,
Nor purposed merit in futurity,
Can ransom me into his love again,
But to know so must be my benefit;
So shall I clothe me in a forced content,
And shut myself up in some other course,
To fortune's alms.[4]

DESDEMONA.
Alas, thrice-gentle[5] Cassio!
My advocation is not now in tune;[6]

---

[1] **hungerly:** hungrily. [2] **the happiness:** the lucky chance. [3] **office:** duty. [4] **So . . . alms:** So I shall pretend to be satisfied and embark on a new career, trusting to fortune's charity. [5] **thrice-gentle:** that is, gentle by nature, by birth, and by breeding. [6] **My advocation is not now in tune:** my advocacy (pleas) will not be well received at present.

My lord is not my lord; nor should I know him,
Were he in favour[1] as in humour alter'd.
So help me every spirit sanctified,
As I have spoken for you all my best,
And stood within the blank[2] of his displeasure
For my free speech! You must awhile be patient:
What I can do I will; and more I will
Than for myself I dare: let that suffice you.

IAGO.
Is my lord angry?

EMILIA.
He went hence but now,
And certainly in strange unquietness.

IAGO.
Can he be angry? I have seen the cannon,
When it hath blown his ranks into the air,
And, like the devil, from his very arm
Puft[3] his own brother;—and can he be angry?
Something of moment,[4] then: I will go meet him:
There's matter in't indeed, if he be angry.

DESDEMONA.
I prithee, do so. [*Exit* IAGO.
Something, sure, of state,—
Either from Venice, or some unhatcht practice[5]
Made demonstrable here in Cyprus to him,—
Hath puddled [6] his clear spirit; and in such cases
Men's natures wrangle with inferior things,
Though great ones are their object. 'Tis even so;
For let our fingers ache, and it indues[7]
Our other healthful members even to that sense
Of pain: nay, we must think men are not gods,
Nor of them look for such observancy[8]
As fits[9] the bridal.—Beshrew me[10] much, Emilia,

---

[1] **favour:** outward appearance. [2] **blank:** the white space in the center of a target—bull's-eye. [3] **Puft:** snuffed out the life of. [4] **moment:** great importance. [5] **unhatcht practice:** treasonable plot that has not yet been executed. [6] **puddled:** muddied; disturbed. [7] **indues:** leads. [8] **Such observancy:** such tender devotion. [9] **fits:** befits. [10] **Beshrew me:** a mild curse.

I was—unhandsome warrior[1] as I am—
Arraigning his unkindness with my soul;[2]
But now I find I had suborn'd the witness,[3]
And he's indicted falsely.

EMILIA.

Pray heaven it be state-matters, as you think,
And no conception nor no jealous toy[4]
Concerning you.

DESDEMONA.

Alas the day, I never gave him cause!

EMILIA.

But jealous souls will not be answer'd so;
They are not ever jealous for the cause,
But jealous for they're jealous: it is a monster
Begot upon itself, born on itself.

DESDEMONA.

Heaven keep that monster from Othello's mind!

EMILIA.

Lady, amen.

DESDEMONA.

I will go seek him.—Cassio, walk hereabout:
If I do find him fit,[5] I'll move your suit,
And seek to effect it to my uttermost.

CASSIO.

I humbly thank your ladyship.

[*Exeunt* DESDEMONA *and* EMILIA.

Enter BIANCA.

BIANCA.

Save you,[6] friend Cassio!

CASSIO.

What make you from home?
How is it with you, my most fair Bianca?
I'faith, sweet love, I was coming to your house.

---

[1] **unhandsome warrior:** unfair assailant (Desdemona is remembering her husband's calling her "my fair warrior"). [2] **Arraigning his unkindness with my soul:** charging him falsely with unkindness. [3] **suborn'd the witness:** caused the witness to commit perjury (as in a court of law). [4] **toy:** whim. [5] **fit:** that is, in a suitable frame of mind to grant a favor. [6] **Save you:** God save you.

BIANCA.

And I was going to your lodging, Cassio.
What, keep a week away? seven days and nights?
Eight score eight hours? and lovers' absent hours,
More tedious than the dial [1] eight score times?
O weary reckoning! [2]

CASSIO.

Pardon me, Bianca:
I have this while with leaden thoughts been prest;
But I shall, in a more continuate[3] time,
Strike off this score of absence.[4] Sweet Bianca,
[*Giving her* DESDEMONA's *handkerchief.*
Take me this work out.[5]

BIANCA.

O Cassio, whence came this?
This is some token from a newer friend:
To the felt absence now I feel a cause:
Is't come to this? Well, well.

CASSIO.

Go to, woman!
Throw your vile guesses in the devil's teeth,
From whence you have them. You are jealous now
That this is from some mistress, some remembrance:
No, in good troth, Bianca.

BIANCA.

Why, whose is it?

CASSIO.

I know not neither: I found it in my chamber.
I like the work well: ere it be demanded,[6]—

---

[1] **dial:** a 12-hour circuit of the hands of a clock. [2] **reckoning:** addition. [3] **continuate:** uninterrupted. [4] **Strike off this score of absence:** that is, make up for my absence (with a pun on Bianca's use of the word *score*). [5] **Take me this work out:** copy this embroidery for me. [6] **demanded:** asked for.

As like enough it will,—I'ld have it copied:
Take it, and do't; and leave me for this time.

BIANCA.

Leave you! wherefore?

CASSIO.

I do attend here on the general;
And think it no addition,[1] nor my wish,
To have him see me woman'd.[2]

BIANCA.

Why, I pray you?

CASSIO.

Not that I love you not.

BIANCA.

But that you do not love me.
I pray you, bring me[3] on the way a little;
And say if I shall see you soon at night.

CASSIO.

'Tis but a little way that I can bring you;
For I attend here: but I'll see you soon.

BIANCA.

'Tis very good; I must be circumstanced.[4] [*Exeunt.*

---

[1] **addition:** credit.
[2] **woman'd:** accompanied by a woman.
[3] **bring me:** take me.
[4] **I must be circumstanced:** I must be governed by circumstances.

Othello
ACT 4

ACT IV

IAGO has pushed Othello's unsettled emotion to the brink of incoherency. Brutally, he feeds Othello's excited mind with images of his Desdemona's treachery and lust. His final stroke is to set up his one piece of supposed evidence as a climax. Othello sees Cassio with his wife's lost handkerchief; he hears Cassio scornfully boasting to Iago of his infatuated mistress. Othello assumes this to be Desdemona. He has received his convincing proof. Cassio is left to Iago to be dealt with, Desdemona he will punish himself. At this point, a legate arrives from Venice, summoning Othello home now that the military emergency is over. Othello seems strangely different to them, and they are astonished at his striking Desdemona in fury. Iago underlines this change to them with hints of foreboding. Othello sets about his revenge. He elaborates a gruesome joke, addressing his wife's maid, Emilia, as a procuress and his wife as a paid whore. His world so dependent on his wife has become a cistern full of loathsomeness and decay. The practical Emilia shrewdly guesses the malice that has led to this nightmare, but not even she dreams it is her husband, Iago, who is the cause. With grim Irony, Desdemona turns to the trusted Iago for advice, but he dismisses it all as an indisposition of Othello's. Desdemona sadly prepares for bed.

ACT IV. Scene I.

Cyprus. Before the castle.

Enter OTHELLO *and* IAGO.

IAGO.
Will you think so?

OTHELLO.
Think so, Iago!

IAGO.
What,
To kiss in private?

OTHELLO.
An unauthorized [1] kiss.

IAGO.
Or to be naked with her friend in bed

---

[1] unauthorized: illicit.

An hour or more, not meaning any harm?

OTHELLO.

Naked in bed, Iago, and not mean harm!
It is hypocrisy against the devil:
They that mean virtuously and yet do so,
The devil their virtue tempts, and they tempt heaven.

IAGO.

So they do nothing, 'tis a venial slip:
But if I give my wife a handkerchief,—

OTHELLO.

What then?

IAGO.

Why, then, 'tis hers, my lord; and, being hers,
She may, I think, bestow't on any man.

OTHELLO.

She is protectress of her honour too:
May she give that?

IAGO.

Her honour is an essence that's not seen;
They have it very oft that have it not:[1]
But, for the handkerchief,—

OTHELLO.

By heaven, I would most gladly have forgot it:—
Thou said'st,—O, it comes o'er my memory,
As doth the raven[2] o'er the infected house,
Boding[3] to all,—he had my handkerchief.

IAGO.

Ay, what of that?

OTHELLO.

That's not so good now.

---

[1] **They have it very oft that have it not:** that is, many persons who enjoy a good reputation do not deserve the name.
[2] **raven:** harbinger of death.
[3] **Boding:** foretelling tragedy.

IAGO.

What,
If I had said I had seen him do you wrong?
Or heard him say,—as knaves be such abroad,[1]
Who having, by their own importunate suit,
Or voluntary dotage of some mistress,
Convinced [2] or supplied [3] them, cannot choose
But they must blab—

OTHELLO.

Hath he said any thing?

IAGO.

He hath, my lord; but be you well assured,
No more than he'll unswear.

OTHELLO.

What hath he said?

IAGO.

Faith, that he did—I know not what he did.

OTHELLO.

What? what?

IAGO.

Lie—

OTHELLO.

With her?

IAGO.

With her, on her; what you will.

OTHELLO.

Lie with her! lie on her!—We say lie on her, when they belie her.—Lie with her! that's fulsome.—Handkerchief—confessions—handkerchief!—To confess, and be hang'd for his

---

[1] as knaves be such abroad: as there are such knaves in the world.
[2] convinced: persuaded.
[3] supplied: gratified.

labour;—first, to be hang'd, and then to confess.—I tremble at it. Nature would not invest herself in such shadowing passion without some instruction.[1] It is not words that shake me thus:—pish!—noses, ears, and lips.—Is't possible?—Confess —handkerchief!—O devil!— [*Falls in a trance.*

IAGO.

Work on,
My medicine, work! Thus credulous fools are caught;
And many worthy and chaste dames even thus,
All guiltless, meet reproach.—What, ho! my lord!
My lord, I say! Othello!

Enter CASSIO.

How now, Cassio!

CASSIO.

What's the matter?

IAGO.

My lord is faln into an epilepsy:
This is his second fit; he had one yesterday.

CASSIO.

Rub him about the temples.

IAGO.

No, forbear;
The lethargy must have his quiet course:
If not, he foams at mouth, and by and by
Breaks out to savage madness. Look, he stirs:
Do you withdraw yourself a little while,
He will recover straight:[2] when he is gone,
I would on great occasion[3] speak with you. [*Exit* CASSIO.
How is it, general? have you not hurt your head?

---

[1] **Nature would not invest herself in such shadowing passion without some instruction:** I would not feel this darkening of my faculties were there not some reason behind it.
[2] **straight:** at once; immediately.
[3] **great occasion:** a matter of great importance.

OTHELLO.

Dost thou mock me?

IAGO.

I mock you! no, by heaven.
Would you would bear your fortune like a man!

OTHELLO.

A horned man's[1] a monster and a beast.

IAGO.

There's many a beast, then, in a populous city,
And many a civil [2] monster.

OTHELLO.

Did he confess it?

IAGO.

Good sir, be a man;
Think every bearded fellow that's but yoked
May draw with you;[3] there's millions now alive
That nightly lie in those unproper[4] beds
Which they dare swear peculiar:[5] your case is better.
O, 'tis the spite of hell, the fiend's arch-mock,
To lip a wanton in a secure[6] couch,
And to suppose her chaste! No, let me know;
And knowing what I am, I know what she shall be.

OTHELLO.

O, thou art wise; 'tis certain.

IAGO.

Stand you awhile apart;
Confine yourself but in a patient list.[7]
Whilst you were here o'erwhelmed with your grief,—
A passion[8] most unfitting such a man,—
Cassio came hither: I shifted him away,[9]

---

[1] **A horned man:** a cuckold (a reference to Desdemona's infidelity). [2] **civil:** civilized. [3] **every . . . you:** i.e., every grown, married man could be in your same predicament. [4] **unproper:** not the husband's exclusively. [5] **peculiar:** to be theirs alone. [6] **secure:** lulled into a false sense of security. [7] **but in a patient list:** within the bounds of patience. [8] **passion:** seizure. [9] **I shifted him away:** I got rid of him.

And laid good 'scuse[1] upon your ecstasy;[2]
Bade him anon return, and here speak with me;
The which he promised. Do but encave[3] yourself,
And mark the fleers,[4] the gibes, and notable[5] scorns,
That dwell in every region of his face;
For I will make him tell the tale anew,—
Where, how, how oft, how long ago, and when
He hath, and is again to cope your wife:
I say, but mark his gesture.[6] Marry, patience;
Or I shall say y'are all in all in spleen,[7]
And nothing of a man.

OTHELLO.

Dost thou hear, Iago?
I will be found most cunning in my patience;
But—dost thou hear?—most bloody.

IAGO.

That's not amiss;
But yet keep time in all.[8] Will you withdraw?

[OTHELLO *retires.*

Now will I question Cassio of Bianca,
A housewife that, by selling her desires,
Buys herself bread and clothes: it is a creature
That dotes on Cassio,—as 'tis the strumpet's plague
To beguile many and be beguiled by one:—
He, when he hears of her, cannot refrain
From the excess of laughter:—here he comes:—
As he shall smile, Othello shall go mad;
And his unbookish[9] jealousy must construe
Poor Cassio's smiles, gestures, and light behaviour,

---

[1] **'scuse:** excuse. [2] **ecstasy:** epileptic seizure. [3] **encave:** conceal. [4] **fleers:** sneers. [5] **notable:** obvious. [6] **gesture:** behavior. [7] **all in all in spleen:** in an overpowering rage. [8] **keep time in all:** be consistent in your behavior. [9] **unbookish:** "lack of learning in the books of love."—Furness.

Quite in the wrong.

Enter CASSIO.

How do you now, lieutenant?

CASSIO.

The worser that you give me the addition[1]
Whose want even kills me.

IAGO.

Ply Desdemona well, and you are sure on't.
Now, if this suit lay in Bianca's power, [*Speaking lower.*
How quickly should you speed!

CASSIO.

Alas, poor caitiff! [2]

OTHELLO [*aside*].

Look, how he laughs already!

IAGO.

I never knew a woman love man so.

CASSIO.

Alas, poor rogue! I think, i'faith, she loves me.

OTHELLO [*aside*].

Now he denies it faintly, and laughs it out.

IAGO.

Do you hear, Cassio?

OTHELLO [*aside*].

Now he importunes him
To tell it o'er:—go to; well said, well said.

IAGO.

She gives it out that you shall marry her:
Do you intend it?

CASSIO.

Ha, ha, ha!

OTHELLO [*aside*].

Do you triumph, Roman? do you triumph?

---

[1] addition: rank; title.
[2] caitiff: wretch.

CASSIO.

I marry her!—what, a customer! [1] Prithee, bear some charity to my wit;[2] do not think it so unwholesome:—ha, ha, ha!

OTHELLO [*aside*].

So, so, so, so:—they laugh that win.

IAGO.

Faith, the cry[3] goes that you shall marry her.

CASSIO.

Prithee, say true.

IAGO.

I am a very villain else.

OTHELLO [*aside*].

Have you scored [4] me? Well.

CASSIO.

This is the monkey's own giving out: she is persuaded I will marry her, out of her own love and flattery, not out of my promise.

OTHELLO [*aside*].

Iago beckons me; now he begins the story.

CASSIO.

She was here even now; she haunts me in every place. I was, the other day, talking on the sea-bank with certain Venetians; and thither comes the bauble,[5] and by this hand she falls me thus about my neck,—

OTHELLO [*aside*].

Crying 'O dear Cassio!' as it were: his gesture imports it.

CASSIO.

So hangs, and lolls, and weeps upon me; so hales and pulls me:—ha, ha, ha!

---

[1] **customer:** one who sells; a prostitute, in this case.
[2] **bear some charity to my wit:** give me credit for having some common sense.
[3] **cry:** rumor.
[4] **scored me:** set a mark, or brand, of disgrace upon me.
[5] **bauble:** plaything.

OTHELLO [*aside*].

Now he tells how she pluckt him to my chamber. O, I see that nose of yours, but not that dog I shall throw it to.

CASSIO.

Well, I must leave her company.

IAGO.

Before me! [1] look, where she comes.

CASSIO.

'Tis such another fitchew! [2] marry, a perfumed one.

Enter BIANCA.

What do you mean by this haunting of me?

BIANCA.

Let the devil and his dam haunt you! What did you mean by that same handkerchief you gave me even now? I was a fine fool to take it. I must take out the work?—A likely piece of work, that you should find it in your chamber, and not know who left it there! This is some minx's token, and I must take out the work? There,—give it your hobby-horse:[3] wheresoever you had it, I'll take out no work on't.

CASSIO.

How now, my sweet Bianca! how now! how now!

OTHELLO [*aside*].

By heaven, that should be my handkerchief!

BIANCA.

An you'll come to supper to-night, you may;[4] an you will not, come when you are next prepared for.[5] [*Exit.*

IAGO.

After her, after her.

CASSIO.

Faith, I must; she'll rail i'the street else.

---

[1] Before me!: an exclamation of surprise.
[2] fitchew: a polecat; a strumpet.
[3] hobby-horse: an abandoned woman.
[4] you may: you must.
[5] when you are next prepared for: that is, never.

IAGO.

Will you sup there?

CASSIO.

Faith, I intend so.

IAGO.

Well, I may chance to see you; for I would very fain speak with you.[1]

CASSIO.

Prithee, come; will you?

IAGO.

Go to; say no more. [*Exit* CASSIO.

OTHELLO [*coming forward*].

How shall I murder him, Iago?

IAGO.

Did you perceive how he laughed at his vice?

OTHELLO.

O Iago!

IAGO.

And did you see the handkerchief?

OTHELLO.

Was that mine?

IAGO.

Yours, by this hand:[2] and to see how he prizes the foolish woman your wife! she gave it him, and he hath given it his whore.

OTHELLO.

I would have him nine years a-killing.—A fine woman! a fair woman! a sweet woman!

IAGO.

Nay, you must forget that.

OTHELLO.

Ay, let her rot, and perish, and be damn'd to-night; for she shall not live: no, my heart is turn'd to stone; I strike it, and

---

[1] **I would very fain speak with you:** I would like very much to talk with you.

[2] **by this hand:** that is, on my oath.

it hurts my hand.—O, the world hath not a sweeter creature: she might lie by an emperor's side, and command him tasks.

IAGO.

Nay, that's not your way.

OTHELLO.

Hang her! I do but say what she is:—so delicate with her needle!—an admirable musician! O, she will sing the savageness out of a bear!—of so high and plenteous wit and invention! [1]—

IAGO.

She's the worse for all this.

OTHELLO.

O, a thousand thousand times:—and then, of so gentle a condition! [2]

IAGO.

Ay, too gentle.

OTHELLO.

Nay, that's certain:—but yet the pity of it, Iago!
O Iago, the pity of it, Iago!

IAGO.

If you are so fond [3] over her iniquity, give her patent[4] to offend; for, if it touch not you, it comes near nobody.

OTHELLO.

I will chop her into messes:[5]—cuckold me!

IAGO.

O, 'tis foul in her.

OTHELLO.

With mine officer!

IAGO.

That's fouler.

---

[1] **invention:** imagination.
[2] **a condition:** temperament; qualities.
[3] **fond:** foolish.
[4] **patent:** license.
[5] **messes:** pieces.

OTHELLO.

Get me some poison, Iago; this night:—I'll not expostulate with her, lest her body and beauty unprovide my mind [1] again:—this night, Iago.

IAGO.

Do it not with poison, strangle her in her bed, even the bed she hath contaminated.

OTHELLO.

Good, good: the justice of it pleases: very good.

IAGO.

And for Cassio,—let me be his undertaker:[2] you shall hear more by midnight.

OTHELLO.

Excellent good. [*A trumpet within.*] What trumpet is that same?

IAGO.

Something from Venice, sure. 'Tis Lodovico
Come form the duke: and, see, your wife is with him.

Enter LODOVICO, DESDEMONA, *and* ATTENDANTS.

LODOVICO.

Save you, worthy general!

OTHELLO.

With all my heart,[3] sir.

LODOVICO.

The duke and senators of Venice greet you.

[*Gives him a packet.*

OTHELLO.

I kiss the instrument of their pleasures.

[*Opens the packet, and reads.*

DESDEMONA.

And what's the news, good cousin Lodovico?

---

[1] **unprovide my mind:** undo my intention.
[2] **his undertaker:** that is, the person who undertakes his punishment.
[3] **With all my heart:** amen.

IAGO.

I am very glad to see you, signior;
Welcome to Cyprus.

LODOVICO.

I thank you. How does Lieutenant Cassio?

IAGO.

Lives, sir.

DESDEMONA.

Cousin, there's faln between him and my lord
An unkind [1] breach: but you shall make all well.

OTHELLO.

Are you sure of that?

DESDEMONA.

My lord?

OTHELLO [*reads*].

This fail you not to do, as you will—

LODOVICO.

He did not call: he's busy in the paper.
Is there division 'twixt my lord and Cassio?

DESDEMONA.

A most unhappy one: I would do much
T'atone them,[2] for the love I bear to Cassio.

OTHELLO.

Fire and brimstone!

DESDEMONA.

My lord?

OTHELLO.

Are you wise?

DESDEMONA.

What, is he angry?

LODOVICO.

May be the letter moved him;
For, as I think, they do command him home,
Deputing Cassio in his government.[3]

---

[1] unkind: unnatural.
[2] atone them: reconcile them.
[3] government: office.

DESDEMONA.
Trust me, I am glad on't.

OTHELLO.
Indeed!

DESDEMONA.
My lord?

OTHELLO.
I am glad to see you mad.

DESDEMONA.
Why, sweet Othello,—

OTHELLO.
Devil! [*Striking her.*

DESDEMONA.
I have not deserved this.

LODOVICO.
My lord, this would not be believed in Venice,
Though I should swear I saw't: 'tis very much:
Make her amends; she weeps.

OTHELLO.
O devil, devil!
If that the earth could teem[1] with woman's tears,
Each drop she falls would prove a crocodile.[2]—
Out of my sight!

DESDEMONA.
I will not stay to offend you. [*Going.*

LODOVICO.
Truly, an obedient lady:—
I do beseech your lordship, call her back.

OTHELLO.
Mistress!

DESDEMONA.
My lord?

---

[1] **teem:** be impregnated.
[2] **crocodile:** an allusion to crocodile tears, which are feigned.

OTHELLO.

What would you with her, sir?

LODOVICO.

Who, I, my lord?

OTHELLO.

Ay; you did wish that I would make her turn:
Sir, she can turn, and turn, and yet go on,[1]
And turn again; and she can weep, sir, weep;
And she's obedient, as you say,—obedient,—
Very obedient.—Proceed you in your tears.—
Concerning this, sir,—O well-painted passion! [2]—
I am commanded home.—Get you away;
I'll send for you anon.—Sir, I obey the mandate,
And will return to Venice.—Hence, avaunt!

[*Exit* DESDEMONA.

Cassio shall have my place. And, sir, to-night
I do entreat that we may sup together:
You are welcome, sir, to Cyprus.—Goats and monkeys!

[*Exit.*

LODOVICO.

Is this the noble Moor whom our full senate
Call all-in-all sufficient?—Is this the nature
Whom passion could not shake? whose solid virtue
The shot of accident, nor dart of chance,
Could neither graze nor pierce?

IAGO.

He is much changed.

LODOVICO.

Are his wits safe? is he not light of brain?

IAGO.

He's that he is: I may not breathe my censure.[3]
What he might be,—if, what he might, he is not,—
I would to heaven he were!

---

[1] **she can turn, and turn, and yet go on:** that is, she can pretend to obey and yet proceed toward her chosen goal.
[2] **well-painted passion:** well-acted emotion.
[3] **breathe my censure:** speak my judgment or opinion.

LODOVICO.

What, strike his wife!

IAGO.

Faith, that was not so well; yet would I knew
That stroke would prove the worst!

LODOVICO.

Is it his use? [1]
Or did the letters work upon his blood,[2]
And new-create this fault?

IAGO.

Alas, alas!
It is not honesty[3] in me to speak
What I have seen and know. You shall observe him;
And his own courses will denote him so,
That I may save my speech: do but go after,
And mark how he continues.

LODOVICO.

I am sorry that I am deceived in him. [*Exeunt.*

SCENE II.

A room in the castle.

Enter OTHELLO *and* EMILIA.

OTHELLO.

You have seen nothing, then?

EMILIA.

Nor ever heard, nor ever did suspect.

OTHELLO.

Yes, you have seen Cassio and she together.

EMILIA.

But then I saw no harm, and then I heard
Each syllable that breath made up between them.

---

[1] **use:** habit.
[2] **blood:** passion.
[3] **honesty:** honorable.

OTHELLO.
What, did they never whisper?

EMILIA.
Never, my lord.

OTHELLO.
Nor send you out o'th'way?

EMILIA.
Never.

OTHELLO.
To fetch her fan, her gloves, her mask, nor nothing?

EMILIA.
Never, my lord.

OTHELLO.
That's strange.

EMILIA.
I durst,[1] my lord, to wager she is honest,[2]
Lay down my soul at stake: if you think other,[3]
Remove your thought,—it doth abuse your bosom.
If any wretch have put this in your head,
Let heaven requite it with the serpent's curse! [4]
For, if she be not honest, chaste, and true,
There's no man happy; the purest of their wives
Is foul as slander.

OTHELLO.
Bid her come hither:—go.

[*Exit* EMILIA.

She says enough;—yet she's a simple bawd [5]
That cannot say as much. This is a subtle whore,
A closet[6]-lock-and-key of villainous secrets:
And yet she'll kneel and pray; I have seen her do't.

---

[1] **durst:** dare. [2] **honest:** chaste. [3] **other:** otherwise. [4] **serpent's curse:** curse put on the serpent for beguiling Eve in the Garden of Eden. [5] **bawd:** procuress. [6] **closet:** private chamber.

Enter DESDEMONA *with* EMILIA.

DESDEMONA.
My lord, what is your will?

OTHELLO.
Pray, chuck, come hither.

DESDEMONA.
What is your pleasure?

OTHELLO.
Let me see your eyes;
Look in my face.

DESDEMONA.
What horrible fancy's this?

OTHELLO [*to* EMILIA].
Some of your function, mistress;
Leave procreants alone, and shut the door;
Cough, or cry 'hem,' if any body come:
Your mystery, your mystery;[1]—nay, dispatch.[2]

[*Exit* EMILIA.

DESDEMONA.
Upon my knees, what doth your speech import?
I understand a fury in your words,
But not the words.

OTHELLO.
Why, what art thou?

DESDEMONA.
Your wife, my lord; your true
And loyal wife.

OTHELLO.
Come, swear it, damn thyself;
Lest, being like one of heaven, the devils themselves
Should fear to seize thee: therefore be double-damn'd,—

---

[1] **Your mystery, your mystery:** that is, go about your duties as a procuress.
[2] **dispatch:** hasten on your way.

Swear thou art honest.

DESDEMONA.

Heaven doth truly know it.

OTHELLO.

Heaven truly knows that thou art false as hell.

DESDEMONA.

To whom, my lord? with whom? how am I false?

OTHELLO.

Ah, Desdemona!—away! away! away!

DESDEMONA.

Alas the heavy[1] day!—Why do you weep?
Am I the motive[2] of these tears, my lord?
If haply[3] you my father do suspect
An instrument of this your calling back,
Lay not your blame on me: if you have lost him,
Why, I have lost him too.

OTHELLO.

Had it pleased heaven
To try me with affliction; had they rain'd
All kinds of sores and shames on my bare head;
Steept[4] me in poverty to the very lips;
Given to captivity me and my utmost hopes;
I should have found in some place of my soul
A drop of patience: but, alas, to make me
A fixed figure[5] for the time of scorn[6]
To point his slow unmoving finger at!—
Yet could I bear that too; well, very well:
But there, where I have garner'd up my heart,
Where either I must live, or bear no life,—
The fountain from the which my current runs,
Or else dries up; to be discarded thence!
Or keep it as a cistern for foul toads

---

[1] **heavy:** sad; unfortunate. [2] **motive:** cause. [3] **haply:** by chance. [4] **steept:** immersed. [5] **fixed figure:** Othello is using the imagery of a clock, and likening himself to a figure on the dial of the world. [6] **time of scorn:** Steevens says this may be compared with "the hour of death," "the day of judgment," etc.; Othello is the central figure at whom the hand of scorn is pointing.

To knot and gender in!—turn thy complexion there,
Patience,[1] thou young and rose-lipt cherubin,—
Ay, there, look grim as hell!

DESDEMONA.

I hope my noble lord esteems me honest.

OTHELLO.

O, ay; as summer flies are in the shambles,[2]
That quicken[3] even with blowing. O thou weed,
Who art so lovely fair, and smell'st so sweet,
That the sense aches at thee,—would thou hadst ne'er been born!

DESDEMONA.

Alas, what ignorant[4] sin have I committed?

OTHELLO.

Was this fair paper, this most goodly book,
Made to write 'whore' upon? What committed!
Committed!—O thou public commoner! [5]
I should make very forges of my cheeks,
That would to cinders burn up modesty,
Did I but speak thy deeds.—What committed!
Heaven stops the nose at it, and the moon winks;[6]
The bawdy wind, that kisses all it meets,
Is husht within the hollow mine[7] of earth,
And will not hear it.—What committed!—
Impudent strumpet!

DESDEMONA.

By heaven, you do me wrong.

OTHELLO.

Are not you a strumpet?

DESDEMONA.

No, as I am a Christian:
If to preserve this vessel for my lord

---

[1] **turn thy complexion there/Patience:** patience itself changes color, or pales, at Desdemona's deceit. [2] **shambles:** slaughterhouse. [3] **quicken:** come alive. [4] **ignorant:** unknowing. [5] **public commoner:** prostitute. [6] **winks:** shuts its eyes. [7] **hollow mine:** the interior of the earth was believed to be hollow in Shakespeare's day.

From any other foul unlawful touch,
Be not to be a strumpet, I am none.

OTHELLO.

What, not a whore?

DESDEMONA.

No, as I shall be saved.

OTHELLO.

Is't possible?

DESDEMONA.

O, heaven forgive us!

OTHELLO.

I cry you mercy,[1] then:
I took you for that cunning whore of Venice
That married with Othello.—You, mistress,
That have the office opposite to Saint Peter,
And keep the gate of hell!

Enter EMILIA.

You, you, ay, you!
We have done our course; there's money for your pains:
I pray you, turn the key, and keep our counsel.[2] [*Exit.*

EMILIA.

Alas, what does this gentleman conceive?—
How do you, madam? how do you, my good lady?

DESDEMONA.

Faith, half asleep.

EMILIA.

Good madam, what's the matter with my lord?

DESDEMONA.

With who?

EMILIA.

Why, with my lord, madam.

---

[1] **cry you mercy:** beg your pardon.
[2] **keep our counsel:** keep this a secret.

DESDEMONA.
Who is thy lord?

EMILIA.
He that is yours, sweet lady.

DESDEMONA.
I have none: do not talk to me, Emilia;
I cannot weep; nor answer have I none,
But what should go by water.[1] Prithee, to-night
Lay on my bed my wedding-sheets,—remember;—
And call thy husband hither.

EMILIA.
Here's a change indeed!
[*Exit.*

DESDEMONA.
'Tis meet[2] I should be used so, very meet.
How have I been behaved, that he might stick
The small'st opinion on my least misuse? [3]

Enter EMILIA *with* IAGO.

IAGO.
What is your pleasure, madam? How is't with you?

DESDEMONA.
I cannot tell. Those that do teach young babes
Do it with gentle means and easy tasks:
He might have chid me so; for, in good faith,
I am a child to chiding.

IAGO.
What's the matter, lady?

EMILIA.
Alas, Iago, my lord hath so bewhored her,
Thrown such despite and heavy terms[4] upon her,
As true hearts cannot bear.

DESDEMONA.
Am I that name, Iago?

---

[1] **water:** tears.
[2] **meet:** fitting.
[3] **How have I been behaved, that he might stick/The small'st opinion on my least misuse:** What have I done that he should find the slightest fault with any possible small misdeed of mine.
[4] **heavy terms:** grave accusations.

IAGO.

What name, fair lady?

DESDEMONA.

Such as she says my lord did say I was.

EMILIA.

He call'd her whore: a beggar in his drink
Could not have laid such terms upon his callet.[1]

IAGO.

Why did he so?

DESDEMONA.

I do not know; I am sure I am none such.

IAGO.

Do not weep, do not weep:—alas the day!

EMILIA.

Hath she forsook so many noble matches,
Her father, and her country, and her friends,
To be call'd whore? would it not make one weep?

DESDEMONA.

It is my wretched fortune.

IAGO.

Beshrew him for't!
How comes this trick[2] upon him?

DESDEMONA.

Nay, heaven doth know.

EMILIA.

I will be hang'd, if some eternal villain,
Some busy and insinuating rogue,
Some cogging,[3] cozening slave, to get some office,
Have not devised this slander; I'll be hang'd else.

IAGO.

Fie, there is no such man; it is impossible.

DESDEMONA.

If any such there be, heaven pardon him!

---

[1] callet: strumpet.
[2] trick: illusion.
[3] cogging: cheating.

EMILIA.

A halter[1] pardon him! and hell gnaw his bones!
Why should he call her whore? who keeps her company?
What place? what time? what form? what likelihood?
The Moor's abused [2] by some most villainous knave,
Some base notorious[3] knave, some scurvy fellow:—
O heaven, that such companions[4] thou'ldst unfold,[5]
And put in every honest hand a whip
To lash the rascals naked through the world
Even from the east to th'west!

IAGO.

Speak within door.[6]

EMILIA.

O, fie upon them! Some such squire he was
That turn'd your wit the seamy side without,[7]
And made you to suspect me with the Moor.

IAGO.

You are a fool; go to.

DESDEMONA.

O good Iago,
What shall I do to win my lord again?
Good friend, go to him; for, by this light of heaven,
I know not how I lost him. Here I kneel:—
If e'er my will did trespass 'gainst his love,
Either in discourse of thought or actual deed;
Or that mine eyes, mine ears, or any sense,
Delighted them in any other form;
Or that I do not yet, and ever did,

---

[1] **halter:** hangman's noose. [2] **abused:** deceived. [3] **notorious:** gross: [4] **companions:** rogues; fellows. [5] **unfold:** expose. [6] **Speak within door:** mind your tongue; speak more rationally. [7] **the seamy side without:** inside out

And ever will—though he do shake me off
To beggarly divorcement—love him dearly,
Comfort forswear me! Unkindness may do much;
And his unkindness may defeat my life,
But never taint my love. I cannot say 'whore,'—
It does abhor me[1] now I speak the word;
To do the act that might the addition[2] earn
Not the world's mass of vanity[3] could make me.

IAGO.

I pray you, be content:[4] 'tis but his humour:
The business of the state does him offence,
And he does chide with you.

DESDEMONA.

If 'twere no other,—

IAGO.

'Tis but so, I warrant.

[*Trumpets within.*

Hark, how these instruments summon to supper!
The messengers of Venice stay the meat:[5]
Go in, and weep not; all things shall be well.

[*Exeunt* DESDEMONA *and* EMILIA.

Enter RODERIGO.

How now, Roderigo!

RODERIGO.

I do not find that thou deal'st justly with me.

IAGO.

What in the contrary?

RODERIGO.

Every day thou daff'st me[6] with some device, Iago; and rather, as it seems to me now, keep'st from me all conveniency[7] than[8] suppliest me with the least advantage of hope. I will, indeed, no longer endure it; nor am I yet persuaded to put up in peace what already I have foolishly suffer'd.

---

[1] **It does abhor me:** it is abhorrent to me. [2] **addition:** title. [3] **vanity:** splendor; finery. [4] **be content:** put your mind at ease. [5] **stay the meat:** await the meal, or supper. [6] **daff'st me:** put me off. [7] **conveniency:** opportunity. [8] **than:** that.

IAGO.

Will you hear me, Roderigo?

RODERIGO.

Faith, I have heard too much; for your words and performances are no kin together.

IAGO.

You charge me most unjustly.

RODERIGO.

With naught but truth. I have wasted myself out of my means. The jewels you have had from me to deliver to Desdemona would half have corrupted a votarist:[1] you have told me she hath received them, and return'd me expectations and comforts of sudden respect and acquaintance; but I find none.

IAGO.

Well; go to; very well.

RODERIGO.

Very well! go to! I cannot go to, man; nor 'tis not very well: nay, I think it is scurvy, and begin to find myself fopt[2] in it.

IAGO.

Very well.

RODERIGO.

I tell you 'tis not very well. I will make myself known to Desdemona: if she will return me my jewels, I will give over my suit, and repent my unlawful solicitation; if not, assure yourself I will seek satisfaction of you.

IAGO.

You have said now.[3]

RODERIGO.

Ay, and said nothing but what I protest intendment of doing.

---

[1] **votarist:** nun.
[2] **fopt:** duped; made a fool of.
[3] **You have said now:** you have had your say.

IAGO.

Why, now I see there's mettle in thee; and even from this instant do build on thee a better opinion than ever before. Give me thy hand, Roderigo: thou hast taken against me a most just exception; but yet, I protest, I have dealt most directly[1] in thy affair.

RODERIGO.

It hath not appear'd.

IAGO.

I grant, indeed, it hath not appear'd; and your suspicion is not without wit and judgement. But, Roderigo, if thou hast that in thee indeed, which I have greater reason to believe now than ever,—I mean purpose, courage, and valour,—this night show it: if thou the next night following enjoy not Desdemona, take me from this world with treachery, and devise engines[2] for my life.

RODERIGO.

Well, what is it? is it within reason and compass? [3]

IAGO.

Sir, there is especial commission come from Venice to depute Cassio in Othello's place.

RODERIGO.

Is that true? why, then Othello and Desdemona return again to Venice.

IAGO.

O, no; he goes into Mauritania, and takes away with him the fair Desdemona, unless his abode be linger'd here by some accident: wherein none can be so determinate as the removing of Cassio.

---

[1] directly: straightforwardly.
[2] engines: methods of torture.
[3] compass: the realm of possibility.

RODERIGO.

How do you mean, removing of him?

IAGO.

Why, by making him uncapable of Othello's place,—knocking out his brains.

RODERIGO.

And that you would have me to do?

IAGO.

Ay, if you dare do yourself a profit and a right. He sups to-night with a harlotry,[1] and thither will I go to him:—he knows not yet of his honourable fortune. If you will watch his going thence,—which I will fashion to fall out between twelve and one,—you may take him[2] at your pleasure: I will be near to second your attempt, and he shall fall between us. Come, stand not amazed [3] at it, but go along with me; I will show you such a necessity in his death, that you shall think yourself bound to put it on him. It is now high supper-time,[4] and the night grows to waste:[5] about it.

RODERIGO.

I will hear further reason for this.

IAGO.

And you shall be satisfied. [*Exeunt.*

SCENE III.

Another room in the castle.

Enter OTHELLO, LODOVICO, DESDEMONA, EMILIA, *and* ATTENDANTS.

LODOVICO.

I do beseech you, sir, trouble yourself no further.

---

[1] **harlotry:** wench.
[2] **take him:** surprise him.
[3] **amazed:** as though struck dumb.
[4] **high supper-time:** that is, full time.
[5] **grows to waste:** is wasting.

OTHELLO.

O, pardon me; 'twill do me good to walk.

LODOVICO.

Madam, good night; I humbly thank your ladyship.

DESDEMONA.

Your honour is most welcome.

OTHELLO.

Will you walk, sir?

O,—Desdemona,—

DESDEMONA.

My lord?

OTHELLO.

Get you to bed on th'instant; I will be return'd forthwith: dismiss your attendant there: look't be done.

DESDEMONA.

I will, my lord.

[*Exeunt* OTHELLO, LODOVICO, *and* ATTENDANTS.

EMILIA.

How goes it now? he looks gentler than he did.

DESDEMONA.

He says he will return incontinent:[1]
He hath commanded me to go to bed,
And bade me to dismiss you.

EMILIA.

Dismiss me!

DESDEMONA.

It was his bidding; therefore, good Emilia,
Give me my nightly wearing, and adieu:
We must not now displease him.

---

[1] **incontinent:** immediately.

EMILIA.

I would you had never seen him!

DESDEMONA.

So would not I: my love doth so approve him,
That even his stubbornness,[1] his checks,[2] his frowns,—
Prithee, unpin me,—have grace and favour in them.

EMILIA.

I have laid those sheets you bade me on the bed.

DESDEMONA.

All's one.[3]—Good faith, how foolish are our minds!—
If I do die before thee, prithee, shroud me
In one of those same sheets.

EMILIA.

Come, come, you talk.[4]

DESDEMONA.

My mother had a maid call'd Barbara:
She was in love; and he she loved proved mad,
And did forsake her: she had a song of 'willow;'
An old thing 'twas, but it exprest her fortune,
And she died singing it: that song to-night
Will not go from my mind; I have much to do,
But to go hang my head all at one side,
And sing it like poor Barbara.—Prithee, dispatch.

EMILIA.

Shall I go fetch your night-gown?

DESDEMONA.

No, unpin me here.—
This Lodovico is a proper man.

EMILIA.

A very handsome man.

---

[1] **stubbornness:** refusal to believe her (Desdemona) faithful.
[2] **checks:** rebukes.
[3] **All's one:** it does not matter.
[4] **you talk:** you prattle.

DESDEMONA.

He speaks well.

EMILIA.

I know a lady in Venice would have walkt barefoot to Palestine[1] for a touch of his nether[2] lip.

DESDEMONA [*singing*].

The poor soul sat sighing by a sycamore tree,
Sing all a green willow;
Her hand on her bosom, her head on her knee,
Sing willow, willow, willow:
The fresh streams ran by her, and murmur'd her moans;
Sing willow, willow, willow;
Her salt tears fell from her, and soften'd the stones;—
Lay by these:—
Sing willow, willow, willow;
Prithee, hie thee; he'll come anon:—
Sing all a green willow must be my garland.
Let nobody blame him; his scorn I approve,—
Nay, that's not next.—Hark! who is't that knocks?

EMILIA.

It is the wind.

DESDEMONA.

I call'd my love false love; but what said he then?
Sing willow, willow, willow;
If I court moe[3] women, you'll couch with moe men.—
So, get thee gone; good night. Mine eyes do itch;
Doth that bode weeping?

EMILIA.

'Tis neither here nor there.[4]

---

[1] **walkt barefoot to Palestine:** made a pilgrimage to Palestine.
[2] **nether:** lower.
[3] **moe:** more.
[4] **'Tis neither here nor there:** it has no special meaning (an expression which is still in use today).

DESDEMONA.

I have heard it said so.—O, these men, these men!—
Dost thou in conscience think,—tell me, Emilia,—
That there be women do abuse[1] their husbands
In such gross kind?

EMILIA.

There be some such, no question.

DESDEMONA.

Wouldst thou do such a deed for all the world?

EMILIA.

Why, would not you?

DESDEMONA.

No, by this heavenly light! [2]

EMILIA.

Nor I neither by this heavenly light; I might do't as well i'th'dark.

DESDEMONA.

Wouldst thou do such a deed for all the world?

EMILIA.

The world is a huge thing: it is a great price for a small vice.

DESDEMONA.

In troth, I think thou wouldst not.

EMILIA.

In troth, I think I should; and undo't when I had done. Marry, I would not do such a thing for a joint-ring,[3] nor for measures of lawn, nor for gowns, petticoats, nor caps, nor any petty exhibition;[4] but, for the whole world,—why, who would not make her husband a cuckold to make him a monarch? I should venture purgatory for't.

---

[1] **abuse:** deceive.
[2] **by this heavenly light:** a mild oath.
[3] **joint-ring:** a ring with two interlocking halves (a love token).
[4] **exhibition:** allowance; pension.

DESDEMONA.

Beshrew me, if I would do such a wrong
For the whole world.

EMILIA.

Why, the wrong is but a wrong i'th'world; and having the world for your labour, 'tis a wrong in your own world, and you might quickly make it right.

DESDEMONA.

I do not think there is any such woman.

EMILIA.

Yes, a dozen; and as many to th'vantage[1] as would store the world they play'd for.
But I do think it is their husbands' faults
If wives do fall: say that they slack their duties,
And pour our treasures into foreign[2] laps;
Or else break out in peevish[3] jealousies,
Throwing restraint upon us; or say they strike us,
Or scant our former having in despite;[4]
Why, we have galls;[5] and though we have some grace,[6]
Yet have we some revenge. Let husbands know
Their wives have sense like them: they see, and smell,
And have their palates both for sweet and sour,
As husbands have. What is it that they do
When they change us for others? Is it sport?
I think it is: and doth affection breed it?
I think it doth: is't frailty that thus errs?
It is so too:—and have not we affections,
Desires for sport, and frailty, as men have?
Then let them use us well: else let them know,
The ills we do, their ills instruct us so.

---

[1] **to th'vantage**: in addition; to boot. [2] **foreign**: alien. [3] **peevish**: silly. [4] **scant our former having in despite**: spitefully cut down our household allowance. [5] **galls**: resentments. [6] **grace**: used in the theological sense.

DESDEMONA.

Good night, good night: heaven me such usage send,
Not to pick bad from bad, but by bad mend! [1] [*Exeunt.*

[1] **heaven me such usage send,/ Not to pick bad from bad, but by bad mend:** Desdemona prays that she may, instead of imitating the bad by being bad, become a better person because of misfortune.

Othello

ACT 5

ACT V

IAGO once more makes use of Roderigo, inciting the reluctant dupe to murder Cassio in the night. The attempt miscarries and Iago has to finish off the wounded Roderigo himself to silence him. But Othello, hearing only Cassio's cries, assumes the murder done and goes to his task of revenge. He takes on a double rôle of judge and executioner in approaching his sleeping wife. She awakes and pleads her innocence, but her very horror at the plot against her and Cassio seems to Othello a forced admission of guilt. He smothers her. Emilia bursts into the bedroom with news of the attempt on Cassio's life, to discover the dying Desdemona, still unwilling to blame Othello in any way. Emilia raises an alarm. Othello, in explaining his cruel action to the shocked onlookers, gives Emilia the means to reveal just how totally Iago has duped him. He lunges at Iago but manages only to wound him. The plot Iago has so cunningly worked is unraveled in all its details. Now Othello finally has the truth he has searched for all through the play; in its light, he offers a portrait of his own motives and actions and the consequence of all these—his wife's death and his own. Stabbing himself to complete the account, he joins his wife on the deathbed.

ACT V. Scene I.

Cyprus. A street.

Enter IAGO *and* RODERIGO.

IAGO.
Here, stand behind this bulk;[1] straight will he come:
Wear thy good rapier bare, and put it home:[2]
Quick, quick; fear nothing; I'll be at thy elbow:
It makes us, or it mars[3] us; think on that,
And fix most firm thy resolution.

RODERIGO.
Be near at hand; I may miscarry in't.

IAGO.
Here, at thy hand: be bold, and take thy stand.
[*Retires to a little distance.*

RODERIGO.
I have no great devotion to the deed;
And yet he hath given me satisfying reasons:—
'Tis but a man gone:—forth, my sword; he dies.
[*Goes to his stand.*

IAGO.
I have rubb'd this young quat[4] almost to the sense,[5]
And he grows angry. Now, whether he kill Cassio,
Or Cassio him, or each do kill the other,
Every way makes my gain: live Roderigo,
He calls me to a restitution large

---

[1] **bulk:** buttress.
[2] **put it home:** strike for a vulnerable part of the body.
[3] **mars:** ruins.
[4] **quat:** pimple (a term of contempt).
[5] **the sense:** the quick.

Of gold and jewels that I bobb'd from him,[1]
As gifts to Desdemona;
It must not be: if Cassio do remain,
He hath a daily beauty in his life
That makes me ugly; and, besides, the Moor
May unfold [2] me to him; there stand I in much peril:
No, he must die. But so: I hear him coming.

Enter CASSIO.

RODERIGO.
I know his gait, 'tis he.—Villain, thou diest!
[*Makes a pass at* CASSIO.

CASSIO.
That thrust had been mine enemy indeed,
But that my coat[3] is better than thou know'st:
I will make proof of thine.
[*Draws, and wounds* RODERIGO.

RODERIGO.
O, I am slain!
[IAGO *cuts* CASSIO *behind in the leg, and exit.*

CASSIO.
I am maim'd for ever.—Help, ho! murder! murder!
[*Falls.*

Enter OTHELLO, *at some distance.*

OTHELLO.
The voice of Cassio:—Iago keeps his word.

RODERIGO.
O, villain that I am!

OTHELLO.
It is even so.

CASSIO.
O, help, ho! light! a surgeon!

---

[1] **bobb'd from him:** tricked him out of.
[2] **unfold:** expose.
[3] **coat:** coat of mail.

OTHELLO.
'Tis he:—O brave Iago, honest and just,
That hast such noble sense of thy friend's wrong!
Thou teachest me:—Minion,[1] your dear[2] lies dead,
And your unblest fate hies:[3] strumpet, I come!
Forth of my heart those charms, thine eyes, are blotted;
Thy bed lust-stain'd shall with lust's blood be spotted.
[*Exit.*

Enter LODOVICO *and* GRATIANO.

CASSIO.
What, ho! no watch? no passage? [4] murder! murder!

GRATIANO.
'Tis some mischance; the cry is very direful.

CASSIO.
O, help!

LODOVICO.
Hark!

RODERIGO.
O wretched villain!

LODOVICO.
Two or three groan:—it is a heavy[5] night:
These may be counterfeits: let's think't unsafe
To come in to the cry without more help.

RODERIGO.
Nobody come? then shall I bleed to death.

LODOVICO.
Hark!

GRATIANO.
Here's one comes in his shirt, with light and weapons.

Enter IAGO, *with a light.*

---

[1] minion: darling (a pet name).
[2] your dear: your sweetheart.
[3] hies: hastens toward you.
[4] passage: passers-by.
[5] heavy: cloudy; overcast.

IAGO.
Who's there? whose noise is this that cries on murder?

LODOVICO.
We do not know.

IAGO.
Did not you hear a cry?

CASSIO.
Here, here! for heaven's sake, help me!

IAGO.
What's the matter?

GRATIANO.
This is Othello's ancient, as I take it.

LODOVICO.
The same indeed; a very valiant fellow.

IAGO.
What are you here that cry so grievously?

CASSIO.
Iago? O, I am spoil'd,[1] undone by villains!
Give me some help.

IAGO.
O me, lieutenant! what villains have done this?

CASSIO.
I think that one of them is hereabout,
And cannot make away.

IAGO.
O treacherous villains!—
What are you there? come in, and give some help.
[*To* LODOVICO *and* GRATIANO.

RODERIGO.
O, help me here!

CASSIO.
That's one of them.

---

[1] spoil'd: incapacitated; wounded.

IAGO.

O murderous slave! O villain!

[*Stabs* RODERIGO.

RODERIGO.

O damn'd Iago! O inhuman dog!

IAGO.

Kill men i'th' dark!—where be these bloody thieves?—
How silent is this town!—Ho! murder! murder!—
What may you be? are you of good or evil? [1]

LODOVICO.

As you shall prove us, praise us.

IAGO.

Signior Lodovico?

LODOVICO.

He, sir.

IAGO.

I cry you mercy. Here's Cassio hurt by villains.

GRATIANO.

Cassio!

IAGO.

How is't, brother?

CASSIO.

My leg is cut in two.

IAGO.

Marry, heaven forbid!—
Light, gentlemen:—I'll bind it with my shirt.

Enter BIANCA.

BIANCA.

What is the matter, ho? who is't that cried?

IAGO.

Who is't that cried!

---

[1] of good or evil: friend or foe.

BIANCA.

O my dear Cassio! my sweet Cassio!
O Cassio, Cassio, Cassio!

IAGO.

O notable strumpet!—Cassio, may you suspect
Who they should be that have thus mangled you?

CASSIO.

No.

GRATIANO.

I am sorry to find you thus: I have been to seek you.

IAGO.

Lend me a garter:[1]—so.—O, for a chair,[2]
To bear him easily hence!

BIANCA.

Alas, he faints!—O Cassio, Cassio, Cassio!

IAGO.

Gentlemen all, I do suspect this trash
To be a party in this injury.—
Patience awhile, good Cassio.—Come, come;
Lend me a light.—Know we this face or no?
Alas, my friend and my dear countryman
Roderigo? no:—yes, sure; O heaven! Roderigo.

GRATIANO.

What, of Venice?

IAGO.

Even he, sir: did you know him?

GRATIANO.

Know him! ay.

IAGO.

Signior Gratiano? I cry you gentle pardon;[3]
These bloody accidents must excuse my manners,
That so neglected you.

GRATIANO.

I am glad to see you.

---

[1] **a garter:** support.
[2] **chair:** sedan chair.
[3] **I cry your gentle pardon:** I humbly beg your pardon.

IAGO.

How do you, Cassio?—O, a chair, a chair!

GRATIANO.

Roderigo!

IAGO.

He, he, 'tis he.—[*a chair brought in.*] O, that's well said;[1] —the chair:—
Some good man bear him carefully from hence;
I'll fetch the general's surgeon.—[*to* BIANCA] For you, mistress,
Save you your labour.[2]—He that lies slain here, Cassio,
Was my dear friend: what malice was between you?

CASSIO.

None in the world; nor do I know the man.

IAGO [*to* BIANCA].

What, look you pale?—O, bear him out o'th'air.—

[CASSIO *and* RODERIGO *are borne off.*

Stay you, good gentlemen.—Look you pale, mistress?—
Do you perceive the gastness[3] of her eye?—
Nay, if you stare, we shall hear more anon.—
Behold her well; I pray you, look upon her:
Do you see, gentlemen? nay, guiltiness will speak,
Though tongues were out of use.[4]

Enter EMILIA.

EMILIA.

'Las,[5] what's the matter? what's the matter, husband?

IAGO.

Cassio hath here been set on in the dark
By Roderigo, and fellows that are scaped:
He's almost slain, and Roderigo dead.

---

[1] **well said:** well done.
[2] **Save you your labour:** don't bother with him.
[3] **gastness:** terror.
[4] **Though tongues were out of use:** even if no one could speak.
[5] **'Las:** alas.

EMILIA.

Alas, good gentleman! alas, good Cassio!

IAGO.

This is the fruit of whoring.—Prithee, Emilia,
Go know of Cassio where he supt to-night.—
[*to* BIANCA] What, do you shake at that?

BIANCA.

He supt at my house; but I therefore shake not.

IAGO.

O, did he so? I charge you, go with me.

EMILIA.

Fie, fie upon thee, strumpet!

BIANCA.

I am no strumpet; but of life as honest
As you that thus abuse me.

EMILIA.

As I! foh! fie upon thee!

IAGO.

Kind gentlemen, let's go see poor Cassio drest.[1]—
[*to* BIANCA] Come, mistress, you must tell's[2] another tale.—
Emilia, run you to the citadel,
And tell my lord and lady what hath hapt.—
Will you go on afore?—[*aside*] This is the night
That either makes me or fordoes me quite.[3] [*Exeunt.*

SCENE II.

A bedchamber in the castle: DESDEMONA *in bed asleep; a light burning.*

Enter OTHELLO.

OTHELLO.

It is the cause, it is the cause, my soul,—
Let me not name it to you, you chaste stars! [4]
It is the cause.—Yet I'll not shed her blood;

---

[1] **drest:** bandaged.
[2] **tell's:** tell us.
[3] **fordoes me quite:** destroys me completely.
[4] **chaste stars:** the virgin attendants of the moon goddess (Diana).

Nor scar that whiter skin of hers than snow,
And smooth as monumental alabaster.
Yet she must die, else she'll betray more men.—
Put out the light, and then put out the light:
If I quench thee, thou flaming minister,[1]
I can again thy former light restore,
Should I repent me:—but once put out thy light,
Thou cunning'st pattern of excelling nature,
I know not where is that Promethean heat[2]
That can thy light relume.[3] When I have pluckt the rose,
I cannot give it vital growth again,
It needs must wither:—I'll smell it on the tree.—

[*Kissing her.*

O balmy breath, that dost almost persuade
Justice to break her sword!—One more, one more:—
Be thus when thou art dead, and I will kill thee,
And love thee after:—one more, and this the last:
So sweet was ne'er so fatal. I must weep,
But they are cruel tears:[4] this sorrow's heavenly;[5]
It strikes where it doth love.—She wakes.

DESDEMONA.

Who's there? Othello?

OTHELLO.

Ay, Desdemona.

DESDEMONA.

Will you come to bed, my lord?

OTHELLO.

Have you pray'd to-night, Desdemona?

DESDEMONA.

Ay, my lord.

---

[1] **minister:** attendant. [2] **Promethean heat:** the Titan Prometheus stole from heaven fire to give life to the clay image he had fashioned (man). [3] **relume:** rekindle. [4] **cruel tears:** that is, he is not to be swerved from his purpose by pity. [5] **heavenly:** Godlike, in that, though loving Desdemona, he must punish her.

OTHELLO.

If you bethink yourself of any crime
Unreconciled as yet to heaven and grace,
Solicit for it straight.

DESDEMONA.

Alack, my lord, what may you mean by that?

OTHELLO.

Well, do it, and be brief; I will walk by:[1]
I would not kill thy unprepared spirit;
No,—heaven forfend! [2]—I would not kill thy soul.

DESDEMONA.

Talk you of killing?

OTHELLO.

Ay, I do.

DESDEMONA.

Then heaven have mercy on me!

OTHELLO.

Amen, with all my heart!

DESDEMONA.

If you say so, I hope you will not kill me.

OTHELLO.

Hum!

DESDEMONA.

And yet I fear you; for you are fatal [3] then
When your eyes roll so: why I should fear I know not,
Since guiltiness I know not; but yet I feel I fear.

OTHELLO.

Think on thy sins.

DESDEMONA.

They are loves I bear to you.

OTHELLO.

Ay, and for that thou diest.

---

[1] **walk by:** walk nearby.
[2] **forfend:** forbid.
[3] **fatal:** to be feared.

DESDEMONA.

That death's unnatural that kills for loving.—
Alas, why gnaw you so your nether lip?
Some bloody passion shakes your very frame:
These are portents;[1] but yet I hope, I hope,
They do not point on me.

OTHELLO.

Peace, and be still!

DESDEMONA.

I will so. What's the matter?

OTHELLO.

That handkerchief which I so loved and gave thee
Thou gavest to Cassio.

DESDEMONA.

No, by my life and soul!
Send for the man, and ask him.

OTHELLO.

Sweet soul, take heed,
Take heed of perjury; thou art on thy death-bed.

DESDEMONA.

Ay, but not yet to die.

OTHELLO.

Yes, presently:
Therefore confess thee freely of thy sin;
For to deny each article[2] with oath
Cannot remove nor choke the strong conception[3]
That I do groan withal. Thou art to die.

DESDEMONA.

Then Lord have mercy on me!

OTHELLO.

I say, amen.

DESDEMONA.

And have you mercy too!—I never did

---

[1] portents: fearful signs.
[2] article: act of adultery.
[3] conception: knowledge of your guilt.

Offend you in my life; never loved Cassio
But with such general warranty[1] of heaven
As I might love; I never gave him token.

OTHELLO.

By heaven, I saw my handkerchief in's hand.
O perjured woman! thou dost stone my heart,[2]
And makest me call what I intend to do
A murder, which I thought a sacrifice:
I saw the handkerchief.

DESDEMONA.

He found it, then;
I never gave it him:—send for him hither;
Let him confess a truth.

OTHELLO.

He hath confest.

DESDEMONA.

What, my lord?

OTHELLO.

That he hath used thee.

DESDEMONA.

How? unlawfully?

OTHELLO.

Ay.

DESDEMONA.

He will not say so.

OTHELLO.

No, his mouth is stopt;
Honest Iago hath ta'en order for't.[3]

DESDEMONA.

O, my fear interprets:—what, is he dead?

OTHELLO.

Had all his hairs been lives, my great revenge
Had stomach[4] for them all.

---

[1] **warranty:** allowance; sanction.
[2] **stone my heart:** turn my heart to stone.
[3] **ta'en order for't:** taken measures for it.
[4] **stomach:** appetite.

DESDEMONA.
Alas, he is betray'd, and I undone!
OTHELLO.
Out, strumpet! weep'st thou for him to my face?
DESDEMONA.
O, banish me, my lord, but kill me not!
OTHELLO.
Down, strumpet!
DESDEMONA.
Kill me to-morrow; let me live to-night!
OTHELLO.
Nay, if you strive,—
DESDEMONA.
But half an hour!
OTHELLO.
Being done, there is no pause.[1]
DESDEMONA.
But while I say one prayer!
OTHELLO.
It is too late. [*Smothers her.*
EMILIA [*at the door*].
My lord, my lord! what, ho! my lord, my lord!
OTHELLO.
What noise is this?—Not dead? not yet quite dead?
I that am cruel am yet merciful;
I would not have thee linger in thy pain:—
So, so.
EMILIA [*within*].
What, ho! my lord, my lord!
OTHELLO.
Who's there?

---

[1] Being done, there is no pause: my decision made, there can be no hesitation.

EMILIA [*within*].

O, good my lord, I would speak a word with you!

OTHELLO.

Yes: 'tis Emilia:—by and by.—She's dead.—
'Tis like[1] she comes to speak of Cassio's death;
The noise was high.—Ha! no more moving?
Still as the grave.—Shall she come in? were't good?—
I think she stirs again:—no.—What's best to do?
If she come in, she'll sure speak to my wife:
My wife! my wife! what wife! I have no wife.
O, insupportable! O heavy hour!
Methinks it should be now a huge eclipse
Of sun and moon, and that th'affrighted globe
Should yawn at alteration.[2]

EMILIA [*within*].

I do beseech you
That I may speak with you, O, good my lord!

OTHELLO.

I had forgot thee: O, come in, Emilia:—
Soft,—by and by:—let me the curtains draw.—
Where art thou? [*Opens the door.*

Enter EMILIA.

What's the matter with thee now?

EMILIA.

O, my good lord, yonder's foul murders done!

OTHELLO.

What, now?

EMILIA.

But now, my lord.

OTHELLO.

It is the very error of the moon;[3]
She comes more near the earth than she was wont,
And makes men mad.

---

[1] **like**: possible.
[2] **Should yawn at alteration**: should be split asunder (as in an earthquake or violent upheaval of nature).
[3] **error of the moon**: that is, the moon has strayed from her orbit, and thus caused chaos.

EMILIA.

Cassio, my lord, hath kill'd a young Venetian
Call'd Roderigo.

OTHELLO.

Roderigo kill'd!
And Cassio kill'd!

EMILIA.

No, Cassio is not kill'd.

OTHELLO.

Not Cassio kill'd! then murder's out of tune,
And sweet revenge grows harsh.

DESDEMONA.

O falsely, falsely murder'd!

EMILIA.

Alas, what cry is that?

OTHELLO.

That! what?

EMILIA.

Out, and alas! that was my lady's voice.—
Help! help, ho! help!—O lady, speak again!
Sweet Desdemona! O sweet mistress, speak!

DESDEMONA.

A guiltless death I die.

EMILIA.

O, who hath done
This deed?

DESDEMONA.

Nobody,—I myself. Farewell:
Commend me to my kind lord: O, farewell! [*Dies.*

OTHELLO.

Why, how should she be murder'd?

EMILIA.

Alas, who knows?

OTHELLO.

You heard her say herself, it was not I.

EMILIA.

She said so: I must needs report the truth.

OTHELLO.

She's, like a liar, gone to burning hell:
'Twas I that kill'd her.

EMILIA.

O, the more angel she,
And you the blacker devil!

OTHELLO.

She turn'd to folly,[1] and she was a whore.

EMILIA.

Thou dost belie her, and thou art a devil.

OTHELLO.

She was false as water.[2]

EMILIA.

Thou art rash as fire, to say
That she was false: O, she was heavenly true!

OTHELLO.

Cassio did top her; ask thy husband else.
O, I were damn'd beneath all depth in hell,
But that I did proceed upon just grounds
To this extremity. Thy husband knew it all.

EMILIA.

My husband!

OTHELLO.

Thy husband.

EMILIA.

That she was false to wedlock?

OTHELLO.

Ay, with Cassio. Nay, had she been true,
If heaven would make me such another world

---

[1] folly: unchastity.
[2] false as water: from the Bible—"Unstable as water." Gen. XLIX-4.

Of one entire and perfect chrysolite,[1]
I'ld not have sold her for it.

EMILIA.

My husband!

OTHELLO.

Ay, 'twas he that told me first:
An honest man he is, and hates the slime
That sticks on filthy deeds.

EMILIA.

My husband!

OTHELLO.

What needs this iterance,[2] woman? I say thy husband.

EMILIA.

O mistress, villainy hath made mocks with[3] love!—
My husband say that she was false!

OTHELLO.

He, woman:
I say thy husband: dost understand the word?
My friend, thy husband, honest, honest Iago.

EMILIA.

If he say so, may his pernicious soul
Rot half a grain a day! he lies to th'heart:
She was too fond of her most filthy bargain.

OTHELLO.

Ha!

EMILIA.

Do thy worst:
This deed of thine is no more worthy heaven
Than thou wast worthy her.

OTHELLO.

Peace, you were best.[4]

---

[1] **chrysolite:** a green, semiprecious stone.
[2] **iterance:** repetition.
[3] **made mocks with:** made a mockery of.
[4] **Peace, you were best:** you had better hold your tongue.

EMILIA.

Thou hast not half that power to do me harm
As I have to be hurt.[1] O gull! [2] O dolt!
As ignorant as dirt! thou hast done a deed—
I care not for thy sword; I'll make thee known,
Though I lost twenty lives.—Help! help, ho! help!
The Moor hath kill'd my mistress! Murder! murder!

Enter MONTANO, GRATIANO, *and* IAGO.

MONTANO.

What is the matter?—How now, general!

EMILIA.

O, are you come, Iago? you have done well,
That men must lay their murders on your neck.

GRATIANO.

What is the matter?

EMILIA.

Disprove this villain, if thou be'st a man:
He says thou told'st him that his wife was false:
I know thou didst not, thou'rt not such a villain:
Speak, for my heart is full.

IAGO.

I told him what I thought; and told no more
Than what he found himself was apt and true.

EMILIA.

But did you ever tell him she was false?

IAGO.

I did.

EMILIA.

You told a lie; an odious, damned lie;
Upon my soul, a lie; a wicked lie:—
She false with Cassio!—did you say with Cassio?

IAGO.

With Cassio, mistress. Go to, charm[3] your tongue.

---

[1] **Thou hast not half the power to do me harm/As I have to be hurt:** I can stand more hard blows than you have the power to inflict on me.
[2] **gull:** a person easily fooled.
[3] **charm:** control (compel to be silent).

EMILIA.

I will not charm my tongue; I am bound to speak:
My mistress here lies murder'd in her bed,—

ALL.

O heavens forfend!

EMILIA.

And your reports have set the murder on.

OTHELLO.

Nay, stare not, masters: it is true, indeed.

GRATIANO.

'Tis a strange[1] truth.

MONTANO.

O monstrous[2] act!

EMILIA.

Villainy, villainy, villainy!
I think upon't,—I think,—I smell't;—O villainy!—
I thought so then;[3]—I'll kill myself for grief:—
O villainy, villainy!

IAGO.

What, are you mad? I charge you, get you home.

EMILIA.

Good gentlemen, let me have leave to speak:
'Tis proper I obey him, but not now.—
Perchance, Iago, I will ne'er go home.

OTHELLO.

O! O! O! [*Falling on the bed.*

EMILIA.

Nay, lay thee down and roar;
For thou hast kill'd the sweetest innocent
That e'er did lift up eye.

OTHELLO.

O, she was foul!— [*Rising.*

---

[1] strange: incredible.
[2] monstrous: unnatural.
[3] I thought so then: Emilia is thinking of the moment when she gave Desdemona's handkerchief to Iago.

I scarce did know you, uncle: there lies your niece,
Whose breath, indeed, these hands have newly stopt:
I know this act shows horrible and grim.

GRATIANO.

Poor Desdemona! I am glad thy father's dead:
Thy match was mortal to him,[1] and pure grief
Shore his old thread in twain:[2] did he live now,
This sight would make him do a desperate turn,
Yea, curse his better angel from his side,
And fall to reprobance.[3]

OTHELLO.

'Tis pitiful; but yet Iago knows
That she with Cassio hath the act of shame
A thousand times committed; Cassio confest it:
And she did gratify[4] his amorous works
With that recognizance[5] and pledge of love
Which I first gave her; I saw it in his hand:
It was a handkerchief, an antique token
My father gave my mother.

EMILIA.

O heaven! O heavenly powers!

IAGO.

Come, hold your peace.

EMILIA.

'Twill out, 'twill out:—I peace!
No, I will speak as liberal [6] as the north:[7]
Let heaven and men and devils, let them all,
All, all, cry shame against me, yet I'll speak.

IAGO.

Be wise, and get you home.

EMILIA.

I will not.

[IAGO *offers to stab* EMILIA.

---

[1] **Thy match was mortal to him:** your marriage was fatal to him. [2] **Shore his old thread in twain:** severed his weak thread of life. [3] **reprobance:** damnation. [4] **gratify:** that is, express her gratification for. [5] **recognizance:** token; recognition. [6] **liberal:** freely (and bitterly). [7] **the north:** the north wind.

GRATIANO.

Fie!

Your sword upon a woman?

EMILIA.

O thou dull Moor! that handkerchief thou speak'st of
I found by fortune,[1] and did give my husband;
For often, with a solemn earnestness—
More than, indeed, belong'd to such a trifle—
He begg'd of me to steal it.

IAGO.

Villainous whore!

EMILIA.

She give it Cassio! no, alas, I found it,
And I did give't my husband.

IAGO.

Filth, thou liest!

EMILIA.

By heaven, I do not, I do not, gentlemen.—
O murderous coxcomb! [2] what should such a fool
Do with so good a wife!

OTHELLO.

Are there no stones[3] in heaven
But what serve for the thunder? [4]—Precious[5] villain!

[*He runs at* IAGO: IAGO *stabs* EMILIA, *and exit.*

GRATIANO.

The woman falls; sure, he hath kill'd his wife.

EMILIA.

Ay, ay:—O, lay me by my mistress' side.

GRATIANO.

He's gone, but his wife's kill'd.

---

[1] **fortune:** chance.
[2] **coxcomb:** fool.
[3] **stones:** i.e., stones or bolts of vengeance.
[4] **serve for the thunder:** thunderbolts.
[5] **Precious:** used here ironically.

MONTANO.

'Tis a notorious[1] villain. Take you this weapon,
Which I have here recover'd from the Moor:
Come, guard the door without; let him not pass,
But kill him rather. I'll after that same villain,
For 'tis a damned slave.

[*Exeunt* MONTANO *and* GRATIANO.

OTHELLO.

I am not valiant neither,
But every puny whipster[2] gets my sword:—
But why should honour outlive honesty?
Let it go all.

EMILIA.

What did thy song bode, lady?
Hark, canst thou hear me? I will play the swan,
And die in music:—'Willow, willow, willow.—'

[*Singing.*

Moor, she was chaste; she loved thee, cruel Moor;
So come my soul to bliss as I speak true;
So speaking as I think, I die,—I die. [*Dies.*

OTHELLO.

I have another weapon in this chamber;
It is a sword of Spain, the ice-brook's temper:[3]—
O, here it is.—Uncle, I must come forth.

GRATIANO [*within*].

If thou attempt it, it will cost thee dear:
Thou hast no weapon, and perforce must suffer.

OTHELLO.

Look in upon me, then, and speak with me,
Or, naked[4] as I am, I will assault thee.

Enter GRATIANO.

GRATIANO.

What is the matter?

---

[1] **notorious:** obvious; complete.
[2] **puny whipster:** contemptible whippersnapper.
[3] **ice-brook's temper:** that is, the sword blade was tempered by being put into cold water while red-hot.
[4] **naked:** weaponless.

OTHELLO.

Behold, I have a weapon;
A better never did itself sustain
Upon a soldier's thigh: I have seen the day
That, with this little arm and this good sword,
I have made my way through more impediments
Than twenty times your stop.[1]—but, O vain boast!
Who can control his fate? 'tis not so now.—
Be not afraid, though you do see me weapon'd;
Here is my journey's end, here is my butt,[2]
And very sea-mark[3] of my utmost sail.[4]
Do you go back dismay'd? 'tis a lost[5] fear;
Man but a rush[6] against Othello's breast,
And he retires:—where should Othello go?—
Now, how dost thou look now? O ill-starr'd wench!
Pale as thy smock! when we shall meet at compt,[7]
This look of thine will hurl my soul from heaven,
And fiends will snatch at it. Cold, cold, my girl!
Even like thy chastity.—
O cursed, cursed slave!—Whip me, ye devils,
From the possession of this heavenly sight!
Blow me about in winds! roast me in sulphur!—
Wash me in steep-down gulfs of liquid fire!—
O Desdemona! Desdemona! dead!
O! O! O!

Enter LODOVICO, MONTANO, CASSIO *carried in a chair, and* OFFICERS *with* IAGO, *prisoner.*

LODOVICO.

Where is this rash and most unfortunate man?

OTHELLO.

That's he that was Othello;—here I am.

---

[1] **stop:** defenses. [2] **butt:** limit of endurance. [3] **sea-mark:** marker designating a vessel's destination. [4] **utmost sail:** farthest journey. [5] **lost:** vain. [6] **Man but a rush:** attack only with a reed. [7] **compt:** the reckoning on Judgment Day.

LODOVICO.

Where is that viper? bring the villain forth.

OTHELLO.

I look down towards his feet,[1]—but that's a fable.
If that thou be'st a devil, I cannot kill thee.

[*Wounds* IAGO.

LODOVICO.

Wrench his sword from him. [OTHELLO *is disarm'd.*

IAGO.

I bleed, sir; but not kill'd.

OTHELLO.

I am not sorry neither: I'ld have thee live;
For, in my sense,[2] 'tis happiness to die.

LODOVICO.

O thou Othello, that wert once so good,
Faln in the practice[3] of a damned slave,
What shall be said to thee?

OTHELLO.

Why, any thing:
An honourable murderer, if you will;
For naught I did in hate, but all in honour.

LODOVICO.

This wretch hath part confest his villainy:
Did you and he consent in Cassio's death?

OTHELLO.

Ay.

CASSIO.

Dear general, I never gave you cause.

OTHELLO.

I do believe it, and I ask your pardon.
Will you, I pray, demand that demi-devil
Why he hath thus ensnared my soul and body?

---

[1] **I look down towards his feet:** Othello looks at Iago's feet to see if they are cloven (like Satan's).
[2] **in my sense:** in Othello's miserable state, death is welcomed.
[3] **in the practice:** in the snare, or stratagem.

IAGO.

Demand me nothing: what you know, you know:
From this time forth I never will speak word.

LODOVICO.

What, not to pray?

GRATIANO.

Torments[1] will ope your lips.

OTHELLO.

Well, thou dost best.

LODOVICO.

Sir, you shall understand what hath befaln,
Which, as I think, you know not. Here is a letter
Found in the pocket of the slain Roderigo;
And here another: the one of them imports[2]
The death of Cassio to be undertook
By Roderigo.

OTHELLO.

O villain!

CASSIO.

Most heathenish and most gross!

LODOVICO.

Now here's another discontented paper,
Found in his pocket too; and this, it seems,
Roderigo meant t'have sent this damned villain;
But that, belike,[3] Iago in the interim
Came in and satisfied him.[4]

OTHELLO.

O the pernicious caitiff! [5]—
How came you, Cassio, by that handkerchief
That was my wife's?

CASSIO.

I found it in my chamber:
And he himself confest but even now
That there he dropt it for a special purpose

---

[1] **Torments:** tortures.
[2] **imports:** tells of.
[3] **belike:** doubtless.
[4] **satisfied him:** killed him.
[5] **caitiff:** wretch.

Which wrought to his desire.

OTHELLO.

O fool! fool! fool!

CASSIO.

There is besides in Roderigo's letter,—
How he upbraids Iago, that he made him
Brave me[1] upon the watch; whereon it came
That I was cast:[2] and even but now he spake,
After long seeming dead,—Iago hurt him,
Iago set him on.

LODOVICO.

You must forsake this room, and go with us:
Your power and your command is taken off,
And Cassio rules in Cyprus. For this slave,
If there be any cunning cruelty
That can torment him much and hold him long,
It shall be his. You shall close prisoner rest,[3]
Till that the nature of your fault be known
To the Venetian state.—Come, bring away.

OTHELLO.

Soft you;[4] a word or two before you go.
I have done the state some service, and they know't;—
No more of that.—I pray you, in your letters,
When you shall these unlucky deeds relate,
Speak of me as I am; nothing extenuate,
Nor set down aught in malice: then must you speak
Of one that loved not wisely, but too well;
Of one not easily jealous, but, being wrought,
Perplext in the extreme; of one whose hand,
Like the base[5] Indian, threw a pearl away

---

[1] **Brave me:** attack me.
[2] **cast:** dismissed (by Othello).
[3] **close prisoner rest:** that is, remain a prisoner under close guard.
[4] **Soft you:** wait a moment.
[5] **base:** ignorant.

Richer than all his tribe; of one whose subdued eyes,
Albeit unused to the melting mood,
Drop tears as fast as the Arabian trees
Their medicinable gum.[1] Set you down this;
And say besides, that in Aleppo once,
Where a malignant and a turban'd Turk
Beat a Venetian and traduced the state,
I took by th'throat the circumcised dog,
And smote him—thus. [*He stabs himself.*

LODOVICO.

O bloody period! [2]

GRATIANO.

All that's spoke is marr'd.

OTHELLO.

I kist thee ere I kill'd thee: no way but this,
[*Falling upon* DESDEMONA.
Killing myself, to die upon a kiss. [*Dies.*

CASSIO.

This did I fear, but thought he had no weapon;
For he was great of heart.

LODOVICO [*to* IAGO].

O Spartan dog,[3]
More fell [4] than anguish, hunger, or the sea!
Look on the tragic loading of this bed;
This is thy work: the object poisons sight;
Let it be hid. Gratiano, keep[5] the house,
And seize upon[6] the fortunes of the Moor,
For they succeed on you. To you, lord governor,
Remains the censure of this hellish villain;
The time, the place, the torture. O, enforce it!
Myself will straight aboard, and to the state
This heavy act with heavy heart relate. [*Exeunt.*

---

[1] **medicinable gum:** possibly a gum called "Bernix" (mentioned in *The Great Herbal*). [2] **period:** ending. [3] **Spartan dog:** the dogs of Sparta were notoriously fierce; Shakespeare may also be alluding to the stoicism of the men of Sparta. [4] **fell:** cruel. [5] **keep:** guard. [6] **seize upon:** take possession of.